Children's Media Yearbook

The Children's Media Yearbook is a publication of
The Children's Media Foundation

Director, Greg Childs
Administrator, Jacqui Wells

The Children's Media Foundation
P.O. Box 56614
London W13 0XS

info@thechildrensmediafoundation.org

First published 2017

© Terri Langan & Frances Taffinder for editorial material and selection
© Individual authors and contributors for their contributions

All rights reserved. No part of this publication may be reproduced, stored in a retrieval system, or transmitted, in any form or by any means, without the prior permission in writing of The Children's Media Foundation, or as expressly permitted by law, or under terms agreed with the appropriate reprographics rights organization. You must not circulate this book in any other binding or cover.

ISBN 978-0-9575-5188-6 (paperback)
ISBN 978-0-9575518-9-3 (digital version)
Book design by Jack Noel

CHILDREN'S MEDIA YEARBOOK

Edited by **TERRI LANGAN** and **FRANCES TAFFINDER**

The Children's Media
FOUNDATION

WELCOME TO THE 2017 YEARBOOK 7 Greg Childs	**RESEARCH** **CAN READING IMPROVE CHILDREN'S SELF ESTEEM?** 38 Dr Barbie Clarke and Alison David

WELCOME TO THE 2017 YEARBOOK — 7
Greg Childs

EDITOR'S INTRODUCTION — 9
Terri Langan

CURRENT AFFAIRS AND INDUSTRY NEWS

CHILDREN'S MEDIA FOUNDATION REVIEW — 11
Anna Home OBE

CONCERNS ABOUT KIDS AND MEDIA — 14
Anne Longfield OBE

ANIMATION UK — 17
Helen Brunsdon and Kate O'Connor

JOINED-UP THINKING? UK CHILDREN'S TV PRODUCTION — 20
Jeanette Steemers

ONLINE SAFETY AND AZOOMEE — 23
Estelle Lloyd

FUNK – REACHING OUT TO A FORGOTTEN TARGET GROUP — 26
Margret Albers

BEANO RELAUNCH — 29
Emma Scott

CHILDREN'S CONTENT – ADDRESSING ITS DECLINE IN PUBLIC SERVICE BROADCASTING — 33
Anne Wood CBE

RESEARCH

CAN READING IMPROVE CHILDREN'S SELF ESTEEM? — 38
Dr Barbie Clarke and Alison David

THE REALITY OF VIRTUAL FOR KIDS — 41
Alison Norrington

CAN YOU GROW AN OPEN MIND THROUGH PLAY? — 45
Rebecca Atkinson

RETHINKING TODDLERS AND TV — 47
Cary Bazalgette

FAKE NEWS — 51
Dr Becky Parry

COMING OF AGE ONLINE: THE CASE FOR YOUTH-LED DIGITAL RESILIENCE — 54
Sam Lawyer and Yara Farran

FROM SCREEN TO PAGE: CHILDREN'S MEDIA IN THEIR WRITING — 57
Lucy Taylor

"IT WASN'T REALLY ABOUT THE POKÉMON": PARENTS' PERSPECTIVES ON A LOCATION-BASED MOBILE GAME — 61
Kiley Sobel

CALL FOR REGULATION – CHILDREN'S DATA IN PERSONALIZED BOOKS AND READING RESOURCES — 66
Dr Natalia Kucirkova

GENERAL CONTENT

PROJECT HOPE — 70
Lucy Murphy

OPPORTUNITIES IN THE CHILDREN'S FILM INDUSTRY — 72
Tim Clague

"HUMOUR IS VERY MUCH A SOCIAL, INTERPERSONAL ACT" — 75
Laverne Antrobus

UNBOXING ... A TODDLER'S GLASS OF WINE? — 77
Nellie McQuinn

"WHERE'S SIAN?" – THE IMPORTANCE OF FEMALE FRIENDSHIPS — 79
Katie Steed

VALUES ARE THE NEW BLACK! — 82
David Hallam

EVERYTHING IS THE SAME, ONLY DIFFERENT: THE FUNDAMENTAL NEEDS OF CHILDREN — 85
Katie French

CHILDREN'S DOCUMENTARIES: MY LIFE – ALIVE AND WELL IN A DIGITAL WORLD — 90
Kez Margrie

NOSTALGIA

MUSICAL YOUTH: MY UNLIKELY HEROES OF THE 80S — 94
Chris Banks

AND THEY CALL IT PUPPET LOVE — 96
Warrick Brownlow-Pike

A TWINKLY TIME, LONG, LONG AGO... — 98
Simon Partington

FAREWELL

JOHN NOAKES: A TRIBUTE — 100
Richard Marson

PETER SALLIS: A TRIBUTE — 104
Nick Park

MYKE CROSBY 1961 – MAY 2017 — 105
Karl Woolley

CONTRIBUTORS — 106

WELCOME TO THE 2017 YEARBOOK

GREG CHILDS

This is the fifth edition of the Children's Media Yearbook and the first to be distributed to every delegate at the Children's Media Conference in Sheffield.

It's a proud moment for the Children's Media Foundation. Thanks to the generous financial support of the Authors' Licensing and Collecting Society (ALCS) and Kids Industries, we are able to bring this publication to a much wider audience. We hope you enjoy the mix of information, research and opinion the Yearbook offers. It's an annual snapshot of the state of the children's media industry and the children's and youth audience.

The CMF represents that audience. We act as its advocate, lobbying in Parliament, meeting ministers, civil servants and regulators, responding to public consultations and hosting public meetings. Tax incentives for the creative industries, the future of children's and youth content at the BBC, Channel 4 and the other commercial public service broadcasters, fair regulation of in-app payments, greater emphasis on online safety for children – these are all campaigns we initiated or contributed to – including the idea of a Contestable Fund for Public Service Content, which was originally proposed by the CMF back in 2011.

In a relatively short time, we've changed the nature of the conversation around kids and media in the UK. Politicians now readily accept that children's media matters, whereas in the past they dismissed the idea. They agree that UK-made content is important, because kids deserve to see themselves and hear their own stories, and that in turn helps hold together our diverse society. There has even been progress in getting the press to understand that the arguments about content quality, screen time and the effects of media on the young should be based on legitimate research, not scaremongering.

Members of the CMF Academic Advisory Board have written some of the articles in this Yearbook. We are grateful for that and for their guidance in general. We are also indebted to the other contributors – many from the children's media industry – who make this book such an interesting read and a great record of the children's media year.

Please recommend it to friends and colleagues. Copies can be downloaded or paperbacks purchased at: http://www.thechildrensmediafoundation.org/childrens-media-yearbook-2017

And please help us to help the children's media industry in the UK be the best that it can be. Join as a supporter or patron, or attach your company as a corporate supporter. Our only source of funding is donations from people who are as passionate as we are about the children's audience. Please be one of them. http://www.thechildrensmediafoundation.org/support

Greg Childs
Director
The Children's Media Foundation

CHILDREN'S MEDIA YEARBOOK 2017

EDITOR'S INTRODUCTION

TERRI LANGAN

This is the second year I've edited the Children's Media Yearbook and I wanted to take this opportunity to thank all the contributing writers. They all give their time freely and it is so appreciated.

There is a fantastic range of articles this year with reflections on every aspect of children's content. The book contains the latest thinking on policy, research, business issues and creativity. We look at issues currently affecting the children's media industry such as the Contestable Fund, the "Growing Up Digital" report and the decline of children's content in public service broadcasting. Fake news, protecting children's data and children's self-esteem are just a few of the insightful research topics this year.

There are pieces on Project Hope, Pokémon, Beano Studios and the ever-popular unboxing videos, along with nostalgic articles on how the first sparks of interest appeared from a young age for an animator, composer and puppeteer.

Our back page this year is graced by the indomitable Richard McCourt and Dominic Wood. Dick and Dom will celebrate their 21st year as the favourite duo of children's TV at the Children's Media Conference in July 2017.

Several articles this year reflect content that will be discussed at the CMC, so we're really pleased that the Yearbook will be made available to all CMC delegates this year for the first time. It tells us a great deal about the variety and resilience of the children's media industry in the UK, about the way children's viewing and playing has fragmented onto multiple platforms, and about their continuing passion for content.

CURRENT AFFAIRS AND INDUSTRY NEWS

CHILDREN'S MEDIA FOUNDATION REVIEW

ANNA HOME OBE

Since I wrote the foreword to the 2016 Yearbook, the world in which we live and work has changed dramatically.

Brexit, the sudden departure of David Cameron, the advent of Trump, a snap UK election, and as I write in May 2017, the likelihood of a Tory landslide victory in the June election followed by a potential hard Brexit. None of this appeared to be on the cards this time last year and it will all continue to have an impact on the children's media world.

CMF has been active throughout the year, involved in a number of important policy changes and developments which will affect the children's audience.

The government published its draft proposal on the new BBC charter in May 2016, and after consultation and debate in which CMF took an active part, the final settlement was reached in the autumn. It was less radical than some had feared, although concerns remained about board structure, and the future role of Ofcom as it takes on the regulatory function previously carried out by the BBC Trust.

As far as children are concerned, Ofcom will now set the amount of both hours of transmission and (this is new) the hours of first-run original content for both CBeebies and CBBC. The hours initially proposed are more or less the same as those in 2016. However, it remains to be seen how this system will develop and whether in the future it will result in sufficiently new and varied content for the audience.

More recently, in the last few hours of the final debate on the Digital Economy Bill, Ofcom was given powers to impose quotas on children's commercial public service broadcasters (PSBs – ITV and Channels 4 and 5). In reality, this means a return to the position prior to the Communications Act of 2003, which removed the obligation of commercial PSBs to provide a fixed amount of original children's content.

We have campaigned on this since 2003, first as Save Kids' TV and then as CMF, and have played an important role in keeping the decline in original children's content a live issue.

The final breakthrough came as the result of the recent Save Kids' Content campaign led by Anne Wood (which she writes about in this Yearbook). The campaign was supported by Pact along with many other organizations and individuals. Baroness Benjamin took the lead in tabling an amendment to the Digital Economy Act in the House of Lords which advocated regulation of commercial PSBs, supported by Lord Wood, Baroness Bonham-Carter and others. The amendment in an altered form gained government support and was passed into law at the last minute before the election halted further debate.

This is a great step forward and hopefully will mark a real turning point. However, as always, the devil is in the detail, and how valuable this ruling is will depend on how Ofcom interprets its role and powers; the wording in the Act is somewhat vague and open to a variety of interpretations. It also, of course, depends on the attitude of the commercial companies.

CMF will be working with all the other concerned parties, Save Kids' Content, Pact, Animation UK etc., to ensure that maximum benefit is gained for the UK audience in the future.

Another major ongoing policy issue is the proposed Public Service Contestable Fund which was part of last year's Green Paper on public service broadcasting. CMF has been very involved in the discussions over this – we have had meetings with Matt Hancock, the Minister for Digital and Culture, and with a number of officials at the Department for Culture, Media and Sport.

We held a public event in January to debate the pros and cons of this proposal, and the resulting discussion was both interesting and lively. We also responded to the public consultation (our response can be seen on our website).

Our view is that in the initial pilot phase of this initiative, the funding should be concentrated on the children's sector, rather than spread thinly over a range of public service genres. If it is successful it could be increased and rolled out to other areas. We feel that there is a well-proven case for new investment in public service content for children and it could perhaps be usefully linked to the new obligations of commercial companies (Professor Jeanette Steemers' article in the Yearbook discusses the implications of contestable funding).

We continue to believe that future

funding for this initiative should not come from the BBC licence fee, and that the content commissioned should reflect UK sensibility and culture.

The election has halted progress on all this, but discussions are due to start again in June.

The impact Brexit will have on children's media is as yet unclear. There are concerns that the industry, and especially smaller companies, may suffer from the withdrawal of various European subsidies and funds and restrictions on the free movement of labour. However, others see the possibility of new opportunities opening in the global market.

It is good to see that all three main political parties in the UK election have voiced support for the creative industries in their manifestos and hopefully this support will be forthcoming. All these issues will be discussed in the opening Question Time session sponsored by CMF at the Children's Media Conference in Sheffield in July.

The other major subject of debate in the past year which will continue to be critical is the issue of children and the internet, particularly in terms of online safety and regulation. There has been increasing public and political concern about this and calls for stricter regulation on websites aimed at or easily accessed by children.

The House of Lords published an important report, "Growing Up with the Internet", which among other things proposed the creation of a children's digital champion to be based in the Cabinet office, and that after consultation, the government should develop a new code of conduct for internet providers.

The issue of regulation is fraught with difficulties and conflicting interests. CMF supports and is vocal about the protection of children from exploitation, but legislators need to take care that their solutions are both practical and carefully drafted, and that they are truly acting in the child's best interest.

Professor Sonia Livingstone gave an interesting example of this in a London School of Economics blog, in which she was responding to a European proposal on data protection which would effectively raise the age of children allowed to profile themselves on the internet from 13 to 16. She argues that although this is well intentioned, it could result in limiting the positive value of social media.

We continue to be actively involved in the ongoing debate which will be discussed both at CMC and the Children's Global Media Summit held in Manchester in December.

So, a year of upheaval has brought some positive benefits to the children's media world, and great content continues to be made, but many things are still undecided and unclear. CMF will continue to argue for the best possible content for all children on all platforms.

I would like to thank all our Board and Executive Committee members past and present for their hard work and support, and of course I thank everyone who supports us financially. Please encourage more people like you to join us in the coming year. There is a lot to do!

CURRENT AFFAIRS AND INDUSTRY NEWS

CONCERNS ABOUT KIDS AND MEDIA

ANNE LONGFIELD

The digital world gives children amazing opportunities many of us could never have imagined when we were growing up. Google, YouTube, Snapchat and Instagram are now a part of their everyday lives, offering them a chance to learn, explore and engage with the world. That's not going to change, even if we wanted it to.

It's inconceivable for children to imagine a world without the internet, though for parents it's sometimes hard to keep on top of the rapid technological changes that our kids seem to take for granted. Even the most tech-savvy parents worry.

Despite the internet being something many use at work and at home, many feel out of their depth or unsure about the impact it is having on their children. They want to be sure that it is shaping their children's friendships and their childhood development in a positive way.

Parents accept that they are the first line of protection against the potential dangers arising from the online world, but often think there is more that could be done to support them and their children.

That's why I published the "Growing Up Digital" report earlier this year, following a year-long study by a group of experts in areas like media law, online bullying, safety and children's digital use. Our panel included Baroness Beeban Kidron, who set up the 5Rights project to campaign for better digital rights for children, and Liam Hackett, founder of the anti-bullying organization Ditch The Label. We listened to the experiences of children and parents and set out a range of ideas on how we could give children the three most important skills they need to get the most out of the internet: resilience, information and power.

Like it or not, there's no doubt that kids are spending longer and longer online, even many pre-school children. My five-year-old nephew can navigate his way around his parents' iPad better than most adults could manage. To him it's already an everyday object. This isn't something that we should necessarily worry about, but as children are spending more time in the digital world, and from a younger age, we should be aware that they will inevitably come across some online pitfalls. I was shocked to learn from recent studies that almost a third of 15-year-olds have sent a naked photo of themselves at least once, and that a third of 12- to 15-year-olds have seen hateful content directed at a particular group of people in the last year. Parents understandably worry about chatroom safety and the fear of strangers and grooming, but children themselves are often far more concerned about online bullying or seeing inappropriate pictures of themselves on social media platforms.

In fact, it's clear from "Growing Up Digital" that too many young people feel they don't have control over their social media lives. They are agreeing to complex social media terms and conditions far too readily without any idea of the effect on their rights. In truth, no child could ever be expected to fully understand legal jargon that most adults would struggle to comprehend. So, children are routinely giving up their right to privacy. They are even potentially allowing the content they post – pictures usually – to be traded by the social media giants.

As part of our study, we asked some young people whether they understood the terms of Instagram. It's a platform used by more than half of 12- to 15-year-olds and one in four 8- to 11-year-olds who say that they have a social media account. What was discovered won't surprise anyone. The younger children we showed the terms and conditions to were unable to read more than half of the 17 pages of text. None of them fully understood what they were committing themselves to when they clicked "accept". When we asked an expert in privacy law to simplify the terms so children could understand them, many were shocked by what they read.

Therefore, we need social media companies to rewrite their terms and conditions to make them clearer for children. Sadly, it seems that most are unwilling, which is why later this year I'll be working with legal experts to provide teachers and schools with support aids, so that children have a better understanding of their digital rights. I also hope the government will consider how the data and privacy of children can be better protected in future legislation.

It's important, too, that children know how to report problems on social media sites. Our study found that not all children know how to report unacceptable content or behaviour and when they do, they are usually not happy with the action that's taken. I would like to extend my data collection powers so the children's commissioner is able to oversee the number and type of complaints that social media companies are receiving from children and crucially, what happens to those complaints.

In order to truly address the imbalance of power online, we also need a mediator to act between children and the social media giants. I think we should follow the excellent example Australia has set with its Digital Ombudsman. It would be a role completely independent of the industry, but funded by it, and the job would entail helping children to have content removed from sites if they're unhappy with a picture of a post that invades their privacy, or something is uploaded without their consent or used as a form of bullying.

As the internet and social media become a part of all our lives, it's essential that children are taught from a young age about their rights and responsibilities online. It makes sense for all 4- to 14-year-olds to learn how to get the most out of the digital world, while also being taught how best to avoid some of its dangers. This obligatory part of the curriculum would include what it means to be a responsible citizen online, how to protect one's rights and respect others' rights online, and how to both engage and disengage with the online world.

We know from our research that younger children want to learn these skills, but they sometimes feel uncomfortable talking to teachers and parents about the internet. They would far rather talk to children of a similar age. So, digital citizenship learning should involve younger children being taught by older kids, who they are more likely to trust.

I think it's vital that children are better educated about the internet, that they understand what they're agreeing to when they join social media platforms and that their privacy is better protected. Nobody wants their children roaming around in a world for which they aren't prepared. We wouldn't let a child roam around the "offline" world without teaching them the skills to do so first, so it's time we did more to prepare children for a digital world that has very limited regulation and which is controlled by a small number of powerful organizations.

When it was created 25 years ago, the internet was designed with adults in mind, not children. We know that this is no longer the case and so it's up to all of us – parents, teachers, the government, those working in education and the social media companies themselves, to make sure that every child has the resilience, information and power they need to thrive in the digital world.

ANIMATION UK

HELEN BRUNSDON AND KATE O'CONNOR

"Animation UK will provide the overall advocacy, representation, positioning and influence to support a thriving and sustainable Animation & Visualisation sector"

Animation UK – the bedrock of the animation sector needs you! The continued need for a strong, unified voice has never been more important.

Since Oli Hyatt's article for the last yearbook, the collective aims of Animation UK remain, and a lot has happened on all fronts. Animation UK is now part of an official trade organization and open for business, continuing to collect industry statistics for the government to inform future policy, campaigning for change to benefit our industry, and championing the animation sector to succeed and grow.

As announced at the Manimation conference in November 2016, Animation UK has formed a partnership with VFX, post-production and wider studios and facilities sectors to form UK Screen Alliance. This means we are now working with key sectors from screen across the board (not film and TV) and whilst we know there are operational differences, the overlap and similarities in our businesses mean significant benefits. The combined efforts of this partnership add weight to our voice and can help strengthen the case behind our vision and goals. When we have different issues, we represent animation alone.

Since the Alliance was formally constituted, we have been paying due diligence to setting up a membership structure, finessing a manifesto and fine-tuning a mission statement. We are currently representing large and small animation studios; production companies; animation producers and key supporters, suppliers, distributors, technology and software developers.

A huge thank you must go to the

CURRENT AFFAIRS AND INDUSTRY NEWS

founding companies that have put their monies and time in to support the formation of the organization and agreed to sit on the first Animation Council and wider UK Screen Alliance Board. Aardman Animations; Blue-Zoo; Cake Entertainment; eOne Entertainment; The Elf Factory; Jellyfish Pictures; Lupus Films; Locksmith Animation; Mackinnon & Saunders; Spider Eye and Studio Liddell are amongst the first companies to get the ball rolling. We will continue to set up new working groups as and when required for different issues, ensuring we have secure and solid representation in place. Once we have achieved fuller membership and our initial goals, we will look at elections to the council later in the year.

Our three main topics of focus are business, culture and skills, with an overall mission statement: "Animation UK will provide the overall advocacy, representation, positioning and influence to support a thriving and sustainable Animation & Visualisation sector". Our ultimate objective is to grow the sector in value, size, reputation and reach.

Business: We provide representation on UK policy and fiscal developments and promote the sector globally through advocacy and profile raising

Culture: We promote the cultural value and heritage of animation both in the UK and internationally

Skills: We support the continued development of talent and skills into the sector and will be developing a new skills strategy

Who are we?

We are Kate O'Connor (executive chair) and Helen Brunsdon (director) from Animation UK. Neil Hatton is CEO of UK Screen Alliance and Victoria Johnson is the membership and communications officer. Both Kate and Helen work remotely on a part-time basis, while Neil and Victoria are based at the central London office. So, a small agile team indeed.

Over the last six months

We have made sure animation is on the agenda of all the government departments, as well as partnering and liaising with industry bodies. We have already started to input into policy – the contestable fund, Brexit responses, trade and export responses and the industrial strategy & sector deal to cite a few. We have been growing our knowledge base and making sure we lobby and raise the profile of the sector. However, research is key and we are inputting into new VALUE research, working with the Olsberg cosultancy. This was welcomed at the recent BFI /Animation UK day conference on the South Bank (April 2017) and re-emphasizes the need to track, value and calculate our worth separate to others.

Back in December, we had the unprecedented opportunity to christen the new partnership – thanks to Aardman Animations – at No. 10 and celebrate our fantastic industry in front of VIPs and the Minister of State for Digital and Culture, The Rt Hon Matt Hancock MP. We would also like to congratulate all the award winners in the past year from the various ceremonies as it is truly a great recognition of the UK industry, notably at the BAFTAs, International Emmys and Kidscreen Awards.

What next?

We will continue all the hard work with policy, citing the sector deal and working closely with other key trade bodies to shape new regulation approaches resulting in more children's TV.

In June, we were in Annecy together with a number of our members to promote our work and present a friendly and united face. We are working to reignite our cultural and heritage past, with an aim to seek more funding for initiatives such as short films. We want to join up thinking on archives and support hard working archivists in the UK, to help both studios and independent film makers preserve our past, present and future. Animation UK is becoming proactive in terms of our international presence by attending the main markets throughout the year. We also continue to represent the views of the sector at industry and government-focused events such as Cartoon Business, Westminster Forum and the CMC.

The UK is renowned worldwide for being a pioneer of characters, short films, TV series, specials, games, features and commercials *and* we are an open attractive market for inward investment. But this must be founded through a talent and skills base, and it's a key issue for us going forward. We need to make sure that short-term skills gaps are captured and addressed, and that long-term pipelines are developed, ensuring new apprenticeship initiatives work for us. We need to secure funding for new developments and opportunities. Higher education providers must also be linked to the industry, encouraging and supporting all the hard work which is already happening and being delivered by the likes of the NextGen Skills Academy.

We are working on a membership package with a range of benefits, deals, discounts and developments and our current banding fees are in place. Going forward, we have been tasked to see if we can include freelancers and individual membership packages, so do keep telling us if anything else is needed and we will listen – we always welcome industry feedback! After all, this is Animation UK and industry underscoring the foundations for the future together.

Oli Hyatt is still very much part of Animation UK and is chair of the council. We also congratulate him on his second child and being welcomed back into the fold at Blue-Zoo since passing his duties on. We continue to do our best in following his vision.

Our call to arms has definitely begun so please do help us support our wonderful industry and join Animation UK.

CURRENT AFFAIRS AND INDUSTRY NEWS

JOINED-UP THINKING? UK CHILDREN'S TV PRODUCTION

JEANETTE STEEMERS

After over a decade of declining expenditure and commissioning by UK broadcasters on UK children's productions, three regulatory interventions could provide a welcome boost to UK originations.

First, an unexpected and successful House of Lords amendment to the Digital Economy Bill, approved on 26 April 2017 just before Parliament was dissolved ahead of the election, now gives Ofcom the power to impose quotas on commercial public service broadcasters (PSBs) ITV, Channel 5 and Channel 4. This almost reinstates regulatory powers that were lost in the 2003 Communications Act, precipitating a rapid decline in investment by commercial PSBs, heightened by the junk food advertising ban on ITV in particular. Commercial PSBs reduced their expenditure on UK originations from £59 million to £3 million between 2003 and 2014 (Ofcom, *Public Service Broadcasting in the Internet Age*, Data Annex 2015 London13). The key change of this amendment is that Ofcom can take account of children's "programmes" on all "related services" when it considers quotas, suggesting that provision on CITV, ITV's children's channel which is not a licensed public service, would be sufficient to satisfy any quotas relating to the main ITV channel's public service obligations.

The amendment to the bill, championed by a cross-party group led by Liberal Democrat peer Baroness Benjamin, could be truly significant depending on how Ofcom chooses to use its powers. To implement quotas, Ofcom will have to publish criteria for children's programming on commercial PSBs and carry out a public consultation. After many years of claiming that it had little power to intervene in halting the decline of children's production, Ofcom will finally be able to make a difference, and the way it defines its powers will be crucial.

"Quotas" are not defined in the bill. Transmission quotas (the amount of children's programming broadcast) are unlikely to raise investment in originations as broadcasters could simply show more cheaply acquired or library programming. Output quotas (specifying amounts of original production per year), possibly in threatened genres like drama or factual content, or content for older children, could be more effective, but not if there are only limited funds to back up these production obligations. For example, Australian commercial broadcasters have satisfied origination quotas with lower cost co-produced animation, which is defined as drama, and expenditure on children's content has declined.

Stipulations on expenditure for certain types of programming could have a more profound effect, especially if these are combined with tax breaks such as the current children's programming and animation tax breaks. Evidence from France and Canada suggests that a combination of tax breaks, origination quotas and expenditure quotas can sustain a domestic production industry (Steemers & Awan, 2016). The nature of the quotas will be crucial, as will the ability to apply them to the commercial PSBs' non-PSB services (CITV, E4) and also to non-linear video-on-demand services (particularly important as children's consumption shifts online). Once Ofcom publishes its consultation, stakeholders will need to make a strong case for clearly defined "quotas" that will have a real impact on children's original content.

The second factor that is likely to play a role is whether the UK government, as outlined in its BBC White Paper last year, institutes a contestable fund for public service genres under threat, including children's programming, but extending to arts, regional, minority and religious content.

In its consultation on the Public Service Broadcasting Contestable Fund, announced last December and still under consideration at time of writing, the Department for Culture, Media and Sport (DCMS) floated a number of options for a pilot fund, financed from leftover top-sliced licence fee funding. If the pilot fund is given the go-ahead, it is likely to have £60 million to distribute over two or three years from 2019. The DCMS has yet to deliver its response to the consultation and no one knows how much of the £60 million children's programming will get. A DCMS response is expected in summer or autumn 2017 after the election. Before the Digital Economy Bill "quotas" amendment, a key barrier to the fund would always have been the difficulty of getting commercial PSBs to avail themselves of contestable funding if there were no quotas obliging them to commission original content.

Without quotas, children's content is not particularly attractive or profitable for commercial channels unless they can leverage it internationally through licensed merchandise. Children's programming is simply not profitable enough for UK PSBs. If Ofcom does implement production quotas on commercial PSBs, then a contestable fund for UK-originated children's public service content becomes much more viable, but only so long as the pilot project runs and delivers real quality and entertainment value to children.

The third factor to have an impact will be Ofcom's role in regulating the BBC. Ofcom's current consultation on the BBC's mission and public purpose, with a deadline of 17 July 2017, contains important proposals for BBC children's content, which have to be considered holistically with the previous two interventions. It is proposed that CBeebies has a first-run originations quota of 100 hours per year. CBBC will have annual transmission quotas for news (85 hours), drama (1000 hours) and factual programming (675 hours), stipulations that replicate the existing CBBC Service licence issued by the BBC Trust. What is new is the stipulation that CBBC must meet a first-run originations quota of 400 hours. The originations quotas do not diverge greatly from the 508 hours of first-run originated hours attributed to the BBC in 2015 in Ofcom's 2016 Annual PSB Report. The key change is to the original production quotas, as transmission quotas can be filled with older programming. Again, it is up to stakeholders to make their views known on whether these quotas are satisfactory, and in particular, whether they should be confined to the linear channels, or whether there needs to be some future-proofing that takes account of on-demand platforms and new forms of content.

After the virtual dismantling of the public service children's production ecology in the UK over the last ten years due to regulatory neglect and omission, a trio of regulatory interventions could provide the boost needed by public service children's content. However, it would be wrong to turn the clock back entirely and it is important that any amendments take account of the changing realities of children's media consumption and experiences that are increasingly not linear and not always focused on traditional TV formats.

In the wake of the general election, it promises to be an interesting and eventful year for children's content, and stakeholders need to press for the best possible outcomes for children as well as a sustainable production environment.

This is an amended version of a piece originally published for the Children's Media Foundation newsletter.

ONLINE SAFETY AND AZOOMEE

ESTELLE LLOYD

In certain circumstances, I am a firm advocate that government intervention is needed to influence behaviour. This isn't a popular position but it is not without precedent.

Remember when drink driving was socially acceptable and no one really cared about it? The government recognized the importance of tackling this very serious societal issue and since 1979, up to £3 million a year has been allocated to communicate the problem in very graphic ways. Road deaths and casualties have fallen dramatically from over 31,000 in 1979 to under 8,500 in 2015 and I think it's safe to say that drink driving is now completely taboo.

Earlier this year, the children's commissioner issued a report prepared by the "Growing Up Digital" taskforce showing that children are not being educated or supported for their life online in the same way they are prepared for life offline. Supported by a survey conducted by Mumsnet, it indicates that parents are very concerned about this issue (73% of parents are worried about their children accessing inappropriate content online) but that they are confused about how to address the problem. In addition, many simply do not have the time to work out how their children can be entertained online while staying safe. This excellent report adds to a growing weight of evidence showing how children's childhoods are being dramatically impacted because of what they can access on the internet, and when.

As mobile internet gets faster (thank you, 4G!), household tablet usage spirals with the rise of the low-cost tablet and online homework increases, the problem is not going away. It's the government's job to make sure that the generations of the future are adequately protected. Plutarch said, "a child's mind is not a vessel to be filled but a fire to be kindled." Right now, there isn't space for kindling…

Quite correctly, the children's commissioner has concluded that the government needs to intervene to prepare children for digital life. I am particularly interested in the call for a "Digital Citizenship Programme". This was the reason why Azoomee produced its BAFTA-nominated series *Search It Up* (supported by the NSPCC), an 18-part animated series that shows children how to be smart, safe and kind online in a funny and engaging way.

The report highlights an outstanding parental site called Net Aware, a collaboration between O2 and the NSPCC. This is a great help to parents who are dealing with the problems of social media – cyber bullying, reactions to inappropriate content and much more.

What the report does not push is the idea of establishing a safe place online for younger children (aged 4–9), which would also give parents peace of mind. Think of a playground – all the activities have been designed for children to have fun, test boundaries and make their own decisions as to what they want to do. How high can I go on the swings? Am I brave enough to try the large slide? Can I swing on the monkey bars without falling?

Imagine a single place online where children could watch videos, play games, listen to audiobooks, send safe messages and get creative safely. So much can be learned about model digital behaviour in an environment like this, where children make their own decisions and have fun. As the report makes clear in its opening sentence, "The internet is an extraordinary force for good but it was not designed with children in mind." In a crowded online world dominated by internet giants that want to sell advertising and encourage in-app purchases, this sort of initiative would let children be children online.

As the report further identifies, children accept parental intervention much more positively at a younger age, which is why we strongly endorse the children's commissioner's suggestion that the curriculum starts at four years old. This is also why a safe place online works for younger children.

Much has been said, and rightly so, about the need for improved children's rights online through 5Rights, and the urgent need to amend the UN Convention of the Rights of the Child to reflect the realities of the digital world that we live in today. But why should parents really be worried about their children's data privacy online?

Many adults react very negatively to hearing about their personal data being hawked around and sold without their knowledge. To some extent, we have to accept this will happen as we post on multitudinous social media sites, rely on GPS to get from A to B and increasingly do our shopping online. Nevertheless, it's something that is a major topic of debate today and a growing concern for social media companies looking to maintain their users.

Now, let's think of children. In the UK, the age of consent is 16, a child cannot drive until they are 17 or vote until they reach 18. Under the UN Convention of the Rights of the Child, Article 1 states that a child is a person aged 17 or under. Article 4 of the UN Convention says that it is the government's duty to protect children's rights. Despite this, children well under the age of 17 are expected to make decisions about how their data is used which could potentially affect the rest of their lives. Most children lack the maturity to understand the impact of these online decisions. A harsh conversation gets forgotten over time and so does a fight in the playground, but when you share online, more often than not you live with that shared information (photos, messages etc.) for a very long time.

Is it right that children leave digital footprints before the age of 17 which could potentially affect their ability to get a university place, secure their first job or perhaps secure a bank loan? It's hard to know how this tsunami of personal data is going to be used in the future but to be safe, let's give children a chance to be children for as long as possible. The beauty of being a child is that to a very large extent you can get away with anything… Parents get angry and there are punishments but ultimately, it's all long forgotten over time. It's part of the rich joy of parenting. The internet is less personal, more permanent and potentially less forgiving. I'm all for letting children keep their misdemeanours offline, rather than online.

A version of this article was previously published in the *Telegraph*

CURRENT AFFAIRS AND INDUSTRY NEWS

FUNK – REACHING OUT TO A FORGOTTEN TARGET GROUP

MARGRET ALBERS

Background

In 1997, the children's channel Der Kinderkanal (KiKA) was launched in Germany as a joint venture of the two public broadcasters ARD and ZDF. Discussions about an additional youth channel developed and in 2008, the then MDR Head Udo Reiter made it a conceptual discussion within the public broadcasting system. After much negotiation, in October 2014 the prime ministers of the regions greenlighted that ARD and ZDF should develop content for the target group of 14- to 29-year-olds; content not to be aired on a linear TV channel but online, to reach the target group where they could be found.

To develop the content resources, not of the children's and youth department, but of the "young" radio stations of the ARD, a team was set up to keep in regular touch with the target group, involving all regional broadcasting corporations within the ARD and the ZDF. The head office is in Mainz where a staff of 40 manages the network of editorial departments and producers. The annual budget for the programme with the long working title "Das junge Angebot von ARD und ZDF" is approximately 44 million euros.

What is funk?

Neither its name nor any format details were made public before funk's launch on 1 October 2016. Then, the veil was lifted and the first public service content network started with 40 formats: online-only content on social networks and third-party platforms, including Facebook, Instagram and Snapchat, for 14- to 29-year-olds. Web videos make up 90%

of the content, and established YouTube creators as well as newcomers were given the chance to create content to inform, engage and entertain the community without commercial and political influence or product placement. funk has a public service mandate, which means it has very clear responsibilities according to the broadcasting treaty. Since no user is supposed to be forced to use social media, the entire portfolio is available on the funk website (www.funk.net) and via its app. There, the user also has access to licensed series like *Orange is the New Black*, *Dr Who* and *Class*.

Formats

The portfolio now consists of 60+ social media channels with a remarkable variety. "StarStarSpace" is a quirky animation spoofing popular Space Opera by well-known YouTuber Coldmirror. Fynn Kliemann, do-it-yourself enthusiast and prominent YouTube persona, turns "Kliemannsland", a derelict farm in northern Germany, into a centre of fun, art, music and food. You can follow his progress on YouTube, Facebook, Instagram and Twitter or simply pay him a visit and help out. "Y-Kollektiv" is a group of ten reporters producing Facebook reports on topics like factory farming or illegal refugees in Europe. Since March, funk has helped its younger target group with homework with the "musstewissen" (gottoknow), YouTube channel, which features a different topic each day, from maths on Monday to physics on Friday.

Success

Collaboration with well-known YouTubers and giving young talent a chance has meant remarkable success for funk. In the first four months of its existence, the content network has aggregated 103 million views on YouTube, 44 million on Facebook and a community of nearly 3 million YouTube and Facebook subscribers.

The mystery web series "Wishlist" is a good example of funk's support of talented young people. Marc Schießer, Marcel Becker-Neu and Christina Ann Zalamea pitched their twenty-first century version of Stephen King's *Needful Things*, in which not an antiques shop but an app leads a group of teenagers to their doom.

The team, which has previously created shorts and YouTube channels, were given the green light and a budget of 170,000 euros for 170 minutes of programming. Whilst shooting, they founded their company Outside the Club. The ten-episode series is original, suspenseful, well produced and turned out to be a firm favourite for all – "Wishlist" has 122,000 subscribers on YouTube and is the recipient of a German television award and a Grimme Award (the German Emmy). Furthermore, the series is nominated (with eight other funk formats) for a Webvideo award, the biggest media award in Europe for web videos and social media. The second season has also been commissioned.

It will be interesting to see what will happen in the coming months. Will funk continue to focus on its formats and remain in the background or will it start to become a trusted brand in itself?

Three questions for Florian Hager, managing director of funk

funk was launched on 1 October last year. Wrapping up the first seven months:

What surprised you the most?

"After launching, the thing that surprised us most were the reactions from the community, both in a positive and negative sense. On the one hand, we were confronted with all the hate that YouTube Germany had to offer, amongst other things because we portrayed a young woman wearing a hijab. But reading the discussions in the comment sections under our videos and especially people standing up for us or offering constructive criticism is a really cool feeling. Our biggest learning from this is that you cannot force discourse, but have to let it happen organically through choosing topics that are relevant in and for the community."

Is there a format you are especially proud of?

"Singling out one format is not easy, considering that since October we have launched 60+ social media channels with original content, including investigative journalism formats, the first ever snapchat telenovela and a news bot for Facebook Messenger. However, if I had to choose one it would probably be 'Kliemannsland', a format that focuses on the (granted, slightly chaotic) reconstruction of a desiccated farm in northern Germany and turning it into a playground of creativity, complete with music and art studios, restaurants, room for activities such as wake- and skateboarding and accommodation for people who are interested in joining the project. 'Kliemannsland' embodies so many things that are important to us, such as art, music, our network and a place for a community to come together."

What are the challenges for the next seven months?

"This first year of funk is all about strengthening our network. Since we are not a TV, radio or online channel, it is impossible for users to accidentally zap into our programme while channel-hopping. In order to reach viewers, we need to use Facebook timelines, YouTube videosuggestions, Instagram feeds and Snapchat stories, for which having a network with a strong community plays an integral role. Once we have strengthened our network and built up communities for every format, we plan for the brand to play a greater role within our formats."

BEANO RELAUNCH

EMMA SCOTT

Beano Studios is *the* new entertainment powerhouse for kids (aged 6–106!), inspired by the legendary comic and its brilliant characters. The challenge we've undertaken is to spread the Beano spirit of adventurous, rebellious mischief, where thinking like a kid is celebrated worldwide.

We're powering our mission with a new, free web destination, beano.com; the Beano app; major new broadcast initiatives, plus other expansive projects in the world of film, television, live entertainment, toys, games and clothes. We're going to be loud and proud, sharing our journey via exhibitions and exciting collaborations with some of the world's top creators and brands.

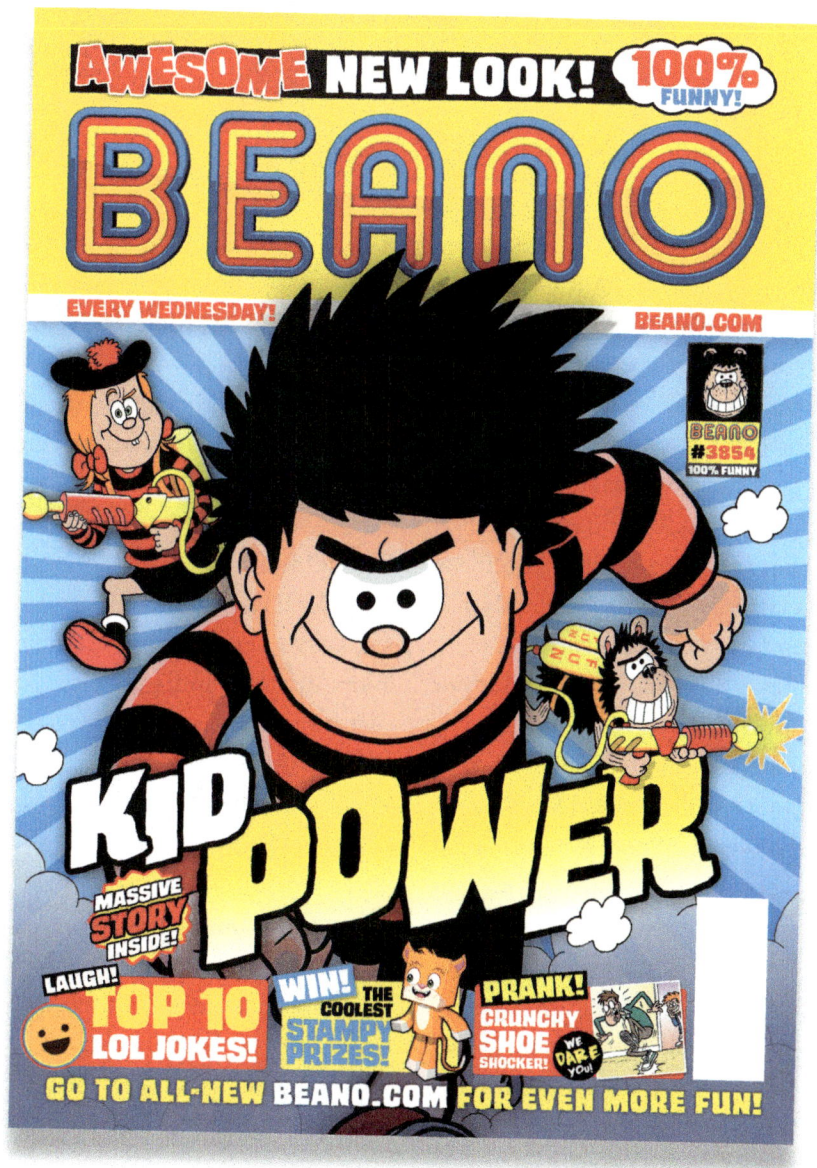

CURRENT AFFAIRS AND INDUSTRY NEWS

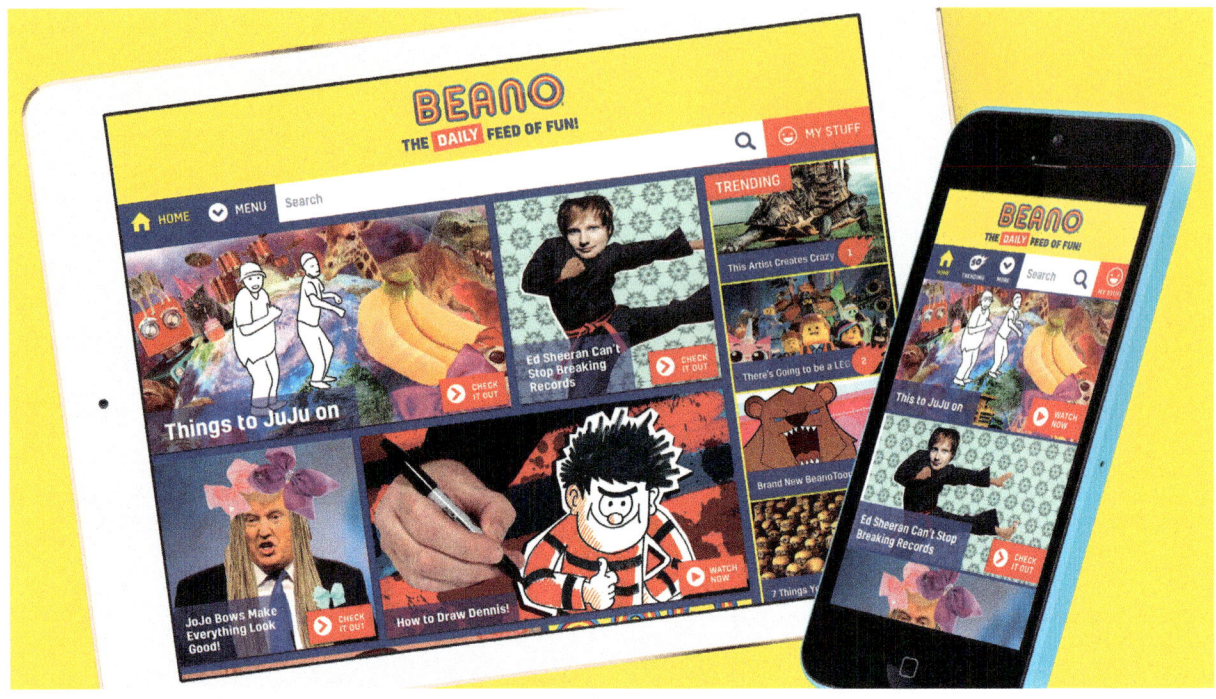

We're creating new, engaging touchpoints every day and, so far, it can all only be described as being "SO Beano".

Let me explain. It's a complicated world out there but we plan to deliver confident clarity and set a new standard of behaviour for everyone. **From now on, any person, thing or behaviour that is inherently awesome should be described as SO Beano – a brilliantly bonkers badge of honour, and a recognition of commitment to sharing the true Beano spirit.**

This spirit has inspired our current metamorphosis from an established publishing force into the fledging, multichannel creative force that is Beano Studios. Our mission? To inspire the whole world – just seven billion people – to embrace the Beano spirit and simply "Think More Kid". Doing so will make everyone feel SO Beano, I promise.

We have expanded our capacity to create more fun, more often for more people. We realized the surest way to achieve this was to share our core comic team's editorial secrets with a larger team of creative geniuses. We needed a bigger Beano boat and we needed to row it even faster.

Our expanded team brings wide-ranging expertise across multiple kids' entertainment formats so they can use the tried and tested, top-secret Beano magic to cast amazing new spells.

Our new talent quickly bought into the baked-in Beano advantage, bought and paid for over nearly eight decades of intense creative development. It's staggeringly simple: **Beano. Knows. Kids.**

It always has. Millions of fan letters and tens of thousands of school visits have guaranteed Beano creators developed an innate ability to "think kid".

I have learned that there is an unwritten contract. To "work" at Beano means committing to a powerful and positive sense of shameless immaturity, enabling you to remain fearlessly young at heart. All I can say is … BOGEYS!

Thinking like a kid isn't rocket science. We've all been one. I assure you that, at Beano Studios, we all still are. But how many "real" grown-ups still regularly try it?

The truth is, it's an attitude that powers everything we do. It's the *way* we think that's fundamental in powering Beano for future generations. We call it the science of "thinkidability". It's sort of a science "fiction", technically speaking, in that we totally made it up, but bear with me as I explain…

Kids have a definitive way of assessing things. They make quick, honest, insightful decisions, without fear or favour. So, Beano or No Beano? *That* is the question! Anyone who thinks like a kid can make that call on *anything*. If you apply it to creating amazing content, products and experiences, it's a powerful tool.

Reflecting on today's entertainment landscape, it's unsurprising that digital is the first area we focused upon. We identified opportunities to quickly expand our reach via entirely free digital services on Beano.com, YouTube, PopJam and social media. What *was* surprising is that we effectively invented an entirely original platform with Beano.com.

Beano.com is our daily feed of fun, designed to make every child feel happier, funnier and more inspired, whether for two minutes or two hours. From original and funny animations, to brand new scripted comedy, boredom-busting makes, viral trends, toy reviews and weekly drawing tutorials, Beano.com is jam-packed with multiple original video strands. It's also bursting with thousands of, frankly, quite random GIFs, illustrations and animations that riff off the hottest playground trends and make our audience (and us) LOL.

We encourage digitally native kids to be active too, giving them the skills to execute the perfect prank, take part in a daily drawing challenge, and flex their brain-power with a range of puzzles, quizzes and polls.

The free app version has some sneaky extra features, such as the prank-tastic Beanocam and a secret sound shake effect – I dare you to try it in one of the quieter sessions this week! Be brave like we have, another tenet of thinkidability.

To attract a new kid audience to the wider Beano experience, we had to move outside the comfort zone of our existing characters and story-telling formats. In widening the range of content we produce, we've been able to engage more kids, who in turn have informed other parts of our development.

For example, girls who weren't already regular readers of the comic told us they expected a wider range of content. Brand awareness of Beano amongst girls aged 6–12 has increased from 42% to 62% since we introduced more variety across both our digital offer and the weekly comic.

Since the launch last September, we've enjoyed an increase in digital downloads of the weekly comic, news stand copy sales and subscribers. Overall brand awareness has also increased across kids *and* adults. We've proudly sponsored *The Simpsons* and *Futurama* on Sky 1 during this period, which has accelerated early growth.

Of course, we also celebrate our much-loved Beano characters across digital, with profiles, comic strips, and heaps of archive video. Plus, if you're really eagle-eyed, you might just spy the brand-new CGI Dennis and Gnasher ahead of their TV debut on CBBC in November

CURRENT AFFAIRS AND INDUSTRY NEWS

2017. It's an eyeball-smacking CGI re-imagination of our most famous characters' adventures, the 52 episodes staying true to the ethos of the comic storytelling, using two former Beano editors as script consultants, with loads of additional hilarious dialogue and visual gags.

The CGI is cutting edge, giving a truly cinematic look and feel. Our production team have produced what they proudly describe as "mini-movies": beloved creations designed to stand up to repeated high definition viewing.

Dennis looks different from the comic, but he's born out of concept sketches by comic artist Nigel Parkinson, who worked with animators on character and background design. Two brilliant new characters, Rubi and JJ, join Dennis on his adventures, and you can read about them in the comic already.

Cinematic CGI delivers compelling eye candy. However, it's the adventurous stories and sheer funniness that make this unique. It's packed with multi-layered humour, so kids of all ages and grown-ups too will find plenty to enjoy.

The expansive scope of the stories has generated exciting play patterns, which our new global licensing program will help fans engage with. There is role-play and vehicles and action figure ranges, as well as the usual pranks and mischievous gadgets typically associated with Beano.

Our growing consumer product range has applied thinkidability to tried and trusted family favourites with brilliant new Beano versions of Guess Who?, Monopoly, Top Trumps and even Cluedo on their way (where pranks played at Bash Street School, rather than deadly weapons, are the new focus!).

Meanwhile, through all the buzz, Beano continues to wow in its original format. A copy is sold every 17 seconds in the UK and Ireland. Almost 400,000 readers enjoy 36 pages of entirely original comic content every week. Over 20,000 faithful subscribers – up 15% year-on-year – can't be wrong when they pay us the ultimate compliment and commit precious pocket money up front.

We've also created the world's no.1 selling annual for nine out of the past ten years. This, despite competition from superpowers like Star Wars and LEGO. Only One Direction sent annual purchasers in the *wrong* direction – and, let's face it, they've not matched us for longevity…

Beano Studios is definitely travelling in the *right* direction, faster than Billy Whizz! Thinkidability is the secret to guaranteeing you're SO Beano. So, try it for free at Beano.com, right now.

CHILDREN'S CONTENT – ADDRESSING ITS DECLINE IN PUBLIC SERVICE BROADCASTING

ANNE WOOD CBE

For most British millennials, childhood memories are interspersed with fond recollections of the television that was dedicated to them. From *Rosie and Jim*, *Teletubbies* and *Fireman Sam* through to *Grange Hill*, *Art Attack* and *Sam and Mark's TMi*, in the 90s and early 00s public service broadcasting offered a truly diverse range of original programming to young audiences. The content was not only enriching, but reflected their native cultural experiences, because it was home-grown. It became an essential component of the British cultural digest.

And yet, the number of new British-made children's programmes has been in sharp decline since legislative changes to advertising rules and public service broadcasting licences were made in the early 00s. The repercussions have been devastating on multiple levels. Not only have children become one of the most underserved demographics in public television, but a vast swathe of the production industry, and thus the British cultural industry, has been affected. As the founder of the Ragdoll Foundation and one of the founders of the Save Kids' Content campaign, I believe the solution must lie in proactive, legislative intervention.

Historically, public service television for children has

always been provided by the BBC, ITV, Channel 4 and Channel 5. The Broadcasting Act of 1990 required commercial public service broadcasters (PSBs) to devote specific amounts of time to children's broadcasting, and this accounted for the healthy level of children's content across the channels which millennials remember. Although this act initially came under fire for posing a potential threat to commercial broadcasters' share of this market, in the end the competition bred by this requirement helped drive both the public and private sector to produce some of their most memorable and commercially valuable content.

The children's production sector subsequently accrued a huge value overseas in selling the UK brand, with global successes such as Channel 5's *Peppa Pig*, CBeebies' *In the Night Garden*, CBBC's *Horrible Histories*, the BBC's *Doctor Who*, CITV's *Adventures of Paddington Bear* … the list goes on. *Teletubbies*, first aired on the BBC in 1997 and one of the frontrunners of this generation of programming, has been shown in 120 countries and in 45 different languages. It generated a reported £200 million in revenue, and sold £50 million in merchandising. It is undeniable that children's television has become a core component of British cultural exports, stimulating the production sector. Moreover, in the words of Professor Jeanette Steemers, "before *Teletubbies*, preschool television was rarely considered a good international prospect." But, as Professor Steemers has argued, "for the BBC these programmes constitute a brand, which has a value in ancillary rights, and a long shelf life, as a new child audience emerges at regular intervals. These shows are also valuable to other public service broadcasters, who on the basis of certain conditions … are allowed to participate from merchandising and licensing receipts."[1] Not only has children's programming strengthened the public image of PSBs, it has given them access to new audiences at home and abroad.

In 2003, the Communications Act downgraded the children's genre from Tier 2 to Tier 3 programming, thus alleviating PSBs of any requirement to broadcast it as part of their licence agreement. Since then, spending on the genre among PSBs has seen an average year-on-year decrease of 13% in real terms, falling from £196 million in 2004 to £89 million in 2015. This decline was compounded in 2006, when Ofcom issued an advertising ban on foods with high fat, salt and sugar levels (HFSS) during children's programmes. Though an important ruling for children's health, the ban further reduced revenues that PSBs could make on newly commissioned or in-house children's content. As a result, less than 1% of the children's television currently available for UK children is made up of original, first-run, British programmes – the rest are repeats and foreign imports.[2]

The decline has created a situation whereby the BBC has the default monopoly on producing children's

---

[1] Jeanette Steemers, "Public service broadcasting is not dead yet – survival strategies in the 21st century", RIPE Conference (Finland, 2002), http://ripeat.org/library/steemers.pdf, p. 8.

[2] Jack Blumenau, "Children's Media Regulations: A report into state provisions for the protection and promotion of home-grown children's media", Save Kids' TV (April 2011), http://www.thechildrensmediafoundation.org/wp-content/uploads/2012/10/SKTV-competitor-territory-research-post-final-updated-24.4.11.pdf

programming, a cosy consensus that has suited providers no longer obliged to commission children's content. In 2015, the BBC broadcasted 82% of all PSB children's programming and 87% of all original PSB children's programming within the UK on its two children's channels, CBeebies and CBBC. Together, CBeebies and CBBC have consistently accounted for over half of all children's output on PSBs since 2002. Conversely, between 1998 and 2015, Channel 4's annual output fell from 971 to 311 hours, and ITV's from 1,005 to 325 hours, just 42 of which were first-run and UK-original.[3] The proliferation of online media platforms over the past decade has also meant that children are consuming an increasing amount of content online, a side-effect of which has been that the concurrent decline in live broadcasting for children has largely been overlooked.

And yet, television viewing remains strong, with 87% of 4- to 15-year-olds still watching live broadcast. Many parents do not have the disposable income to invest in subscriptions to non-PSB competitors, such as Sky and Virgin Media. There is thus an undeniable demand for high-quality children's content among PSBs, and little justification for children becoming one of the most underserved demographic groups. Certainly, online streaming providers are a growing presence on TV screens, particularly in genres that are being underserved by PSBs. But even though the support of independent children's production by online service providers is to be encouraged, PSBs have a responsibility to carry at least equal weight in their provision of children's programming.

Spending on children's programming by pay-per-view platforms, such as Sky and Disney Channel, has also fallen by 40% in real terms since 2004, while Netflix has only recently started to invest in the genre, commissioning just a handful of original British children's programmes so far.

The argument that children's programming threatens commercial PSBs' advertising revenues doesn't hold. ITV's reliance on advertising revenue from live broadcasting is diminishing, as new sponsors and the sale of advertising on its on-demand services have increased. In fact, its revenue from sources other than advertising has increased, from 40% of its total revenue in 2009 to 49% in 2015.[4] In December 2016, ITV also reported a total revenue increase since 2015 of 11% and consistent net advertising revenue of £838 million – a state of rude financial health by any measure, which would leave room for more philanthropic projects. Furthermore, both the creative industry and the government recognize the inestimable benefits of cultural exports in the aftermath of Brexit; evidence of growing markets for British film and television exports from China to Chile suggests that Britain's "soft powers" are worth investing in.[5] And yet, shifts in the culture and mission of PSBs towards a more pragmatic, market

---

3   PSB Annual Research Report 2016, Ofcom (July 2016).

4 Lord Puttnam, "A Future for Public Service Television: Content and Platforms in a Digital World" (June 2016), http://futureoftv.org.uk/wp-content/uploads/2016/06/FOTV-Report-Online-SP.pdf, pp. 46-47.

5 "Brexit Report: The impact of leaving the EU on the UK's arts, creative industries and cultural education – and what should be done", Creative Industries Federation (October 2016), http://www.creativeindustriesfederation.com/assets/userfiles/files/Brexit%20Report%20web.pdf, pp. 49-53.

ideology, wherein "audiences are targeted as consumers rather than citizens",[6] seem to have prevented PSBs from remediating the dearth in content aimed at less immediately lucrative audiences, children among them.

In light of these developments, Save Kids' Content decided that neither children nor the British production industry could wait any longer for market pressures to correct the situation. Given that the government's changes to legislation in 2003 and 2011 had such a significant impact on the landscape of children's television, it was time to seek its support in helping to save the genre's future. After months of campaigning, the Digital Economy Act now includes new powers for media regulator Ofcom which will prove a vital lifeline to the UK's ailing children's production sector. An amendment, originally tabled by the Liberal Democrats' Baroness Floella Benjamin (former presenter of *Play School*), Baroness Bonham-Carter (cousin of the actress Helena Bonham-Carter) and frontbench Labour Party Spokeswoman Baroness Jones of Whitchurch, received the backing of government and is now law. This is a watershed moment for the future of children's television, because the legal change will give the broadcast regulator Ofcom the power to charge PSBs with investing more in UK-made children's productions. This new regulation is designed to make broadcasters negotiate an appropriate settlement for children with the media regulator. The new powers have the backing of the Producers Alliance for Cinema and Television (Pact) and are intended to reverse the significant decline in UK-made children's programmes that has nearly become terminal in the past decade.

The new clause now included in the Digital Economy Bill will provide Ofcom with the flexibility to consider appropriate levels of programming in consultation with the broadcasters, with the help of public and industry consultation. This will, in effect, restore children's programming from Tier 3 to Tier 2 programming, because meeting these criteria will be a condition of PSBs' licence agreements. While the passing of this legislation is cause for celebration, its material effectiveness in reviving UK children's production will depend on the precise conditions Ofcom will set out for PSBs. It will now be up to the children's television industry to come together and ensure that negotiations between Ofcom and PSBs yield as much for the genre as possible. Specifically, this means that the production industry will have to work together with Ofcom to come up with criteria that will push PSBs far enough.

To that end, the Ragdoll Foundation and Pact will be hosting a reception in Parliament on 12 July. This event will be an opportunity to bring parliamentarians and experts from the children's production sector together to celebrate this significant step forward for children's programming, start a dialogue on the scope of Ofcom's new powers, and highlight the economic and cultural opportunities of a revived children's sector.

---

6 Steemers, p. 3.

ALCS is a membership organisation run by writers, for writers.

Since 1977 we have paid over £450m to writers.

Join 90,000 other writers in the UK and across the world and become a member.

Find out more >> www.alcs.co.uk

AUTHORS' LICENSING AND COLLECTING SOCIETY
40 YEARS OF PROTECTING AND PROMOTING AUTHORS' RIGHTS

RESEARCH

Background
Over the past 12 months, 15 diverse families were given the challenge of reading together, to see whether they would be "open" to continuing, and the effects it might have on their children.

Following last year's "Print Matters" report, Family, Kids & Youth and Egmont Publishing teamed up once again, this time to explore whether an intervention, designed to encourage children to read with their parents, would result in a greater love of reading. The project was supported in its early stage by bookseller Foyles.

Concern is frequently voiced over the declining ability of children to read, as their use of tablets and other digital devices increases. The latest research from Nielsen shows that while the children's book market in 2016 was up again year-on-year (+2%), the downward trend of parents reading to their children less continues. In 2016, there was a noticeable year-on-year decline in parents reading to pre-schoolers, and a drop in children aged five and up reading to themselves.

The Reading Challenge Research
Using a mix of ethnography, telephone interviews, focus groups and behaviour change questionnaires, 15 families were recruited in Bristol, Birmingham and Stratford, East London.

Egmont Publishing, one of the best-known children's publishers in the world, wanted to explore, along with

Family Kids & Youth, the effect that an intervention would have in encouraging children and their parents to read. Families with children aged 7–9 (the age at which reading commonly declines) were asked to read together for 20 minutes each day throughout the summer holidays. We visited them at the beginning and end of the holidays and halfway through, the families took part in a "reading challenge" group session in branches of Foyles at each location (Bristol, Birmingham and Stratford East). Each week, families could visit their local Foyles and exchange vouchers for a book, chosen by the child. They found this process extremely helpful, as members of staff were able to advise children on books they might like to read next.

At the beginning of the intervention in July 2016, we asked parents and children to each complete an online behaviour change questionnaire, repeated at the end of the summer holidays. Further interviews were carried out in October half-term, including a behaviour change questionnaire, and again in January 2017. We have since followed the families every two months, and will continue to do so until July 2017, by which time we will have worked with them for over 12 months.

So, what have we found so far?

The families and children taking part in the challenge have found it to be a positive experience, and all 15 families remained with the project from July 2016 through to Easter 2017*. The perceived benefits of reading together include quality time together, with mums often wondering why

they haven't found time to do this before. While some of this tailed off over the hectic Christmas period, all families now make time to include reading in their day. Some parents even reported that they had begun to read novels themselves, and found this a welcome and relaxing experience. At the beginning of the challenge, many admitted to feeling somewhat intimidated by the notion of visiting a bookshop, and reading aloud. However, they were surprised at how friendly and relaxed the visits could be.

Significantly, there has been an increased level of confidence and sense of

RESEARCH

autonomy on the part of the children. This was reflected in feedback from schools, which had a big impact on the children's self-esteem. Both children and parents reported that teachers cited a notable increase in children taking an active part in lessons, a greater willingness to answer questions, and an improvement in reading levels. Children became sufficiently confident to choose their own books, no longer relying on school or parents to make the choice for them.

* just one family has dropped out in this period, due to a family move

THE REALITY OF VIRTUAL FOR KIDS

ALISON NORRINGTON

"To infinity and beyond!"
Buzz Lightyear, *Toy Story*

Stories take us on journeys to faraway lands. From SpongeBob's quirky Bikini Bottom to Harry Potter's Hogwarts; Enid Blyton's ever-changing worlds atop the Magic Faraway Tree to the magnificent Pandora of *Avatar*, stories enrich our world and bring fresh perspectives to the complexities of life. They are fundamental to human growth and critical in child development. Escaping from reality and learning by example through diving into magical fantasy worlds is as old as time.

For decades, we have imagined a future in which we might transport ourselves into a 3D virtual world, and until now theme parks were the place for full, if fragmented, immersion into a story world. Now, technology has finally caught up, offering experiences and stories in virtual reality.

I remain an excited sceptic about VR – excellent story-telling and experience design are challenging at the best of times, and specifically around content designed for children. As someone who has had a series of headsets pushed onto my face over the last three years, only to be overwhelmed, nauseated or disappointed, I was delighted to be asked to be the executive producer of the VR thread at CMC.

The birth of any new industry brings caution along with a "gold rush" excitement and it's important that we responsibly acknowledge that VR for children has arrived. VentureBeat stated in December 2016 that by 2020, global revenue from VR "media entertainment" content will total $2.8billion, and at the VR World Congress in Bristol, Roy Taylor of AMD (Advanced Micro Devices) advised that we all "plan not for where you think VR tech is now, but how it will evolve over the next three years".

Discussion among advocates, naysayers and cautious advisors often focuses on the age restrictions of VR devices. There is a 13+ limitation on Oculus Rift and Samsung Gear, PlayStation advises that children under 12 shouldn't use a PlayStation VR and, whilst there is no age specified for the HTC Vive, there is a warning against young children using one. Google stands by the 13+ restriction for Daydream, advising "adult supervision" when it comes to Cardboard and putting VR into schools with the Expeditions. Whilst there are many reports praising the benefits of VR for children with learning disabilities, along with their educational and therapeutic effects, it's evident that the field requires further discussion, testing and research.

> "Adventure is out there."
> Ellie, *Up*

VR is filled with possibilities, buzzwords and cautionary tales. It's clear we're in a fast-moving industry, but as fast as technology evolves, VR remains a story-telling experience medium in its infancy. Regardless of opinions around kids' use of VR, this *is* happening and there's zero value in sticking our heads in the sand.

The VR sessions at CMC are conversation starters, an attempt to sift the hype from the hip across a trio of sessions to kickstart thinking about immersive technologies and children, policy on VR and kids, creative story-telling and best practice models along with the potential for revenue driving business models. With headset age restrictions and no PEGI (Pan European Game Information rating system) equivalent; the exciting opportunities for animated story world environments and the challenges in creating for children along with hints and tips for exploration, acclimatization, safeguarding and suitability, you can bet there's a lot to discuss.

Beyond the "Empathy Machine": Expectation vs. Reality

Let's get real – the hype of VR as an "empathy machine" is a long shot. VR simply can't elicit true empathy; you can't automate it. VR doesn't remove the problems of gaze, helicoptering and privilege. It can create a sense of temporary confrontation, proximity, and intimacy – all falling short of empathy. However, there's no denying that, done well, VR creates a strong illusion of embodiment, agency and evocation.

As an ancillary story-driven experience to existing IP, Cartoon Network's **I See Ooo** is a VR experience accompanying **Adventure Time**, viewable through Google Cardboard. Framestore launched **Fantastic Beasts VR** to delve into Newt Scamander's magical world, inspired by J. K. Rowling's latest tale. It endeavours to make the user feel like the protagonist: a wizard with a wand in hand, able to cast spells and control the environment.

Google Expeditions offers a more social educational experience as students explore coral reefs, Brooklyn or the surface of Mars through Google Cardboard, taking field trips right from their classroom with their teacher as their "guide". A truly shared VR experience can be seen with **Samsung Bedtime Stories**, allowing parent and child to connect across distance.

As original IP VR story-tellers, Penrose Studios continues to create Pixar-worthy story worlds with shorts **Allumette** and more recently the beautiful **Arden's Wake**, while Oculus Story Studio won the first VR Emmy for Outstanding Original Interactive Program for its short, **Henry**, before closing its doors and announcing that it will no longer create original content, shifting focus away from internal content creation to support more external production.

> "Imagination is the only weapon in the war against reality."
> Lewis Carroll, *Alice's Adventures in Wonderland*

An elegantly designed VR experience incorporates the fundamental pillars of a great story, from set-up to inciting incident, quest, return and resolution across three acts – the timeless form based on structure, pacing and rhythm.

Interactive story-telling tools are baked into a great VR experience along with additional theories from architecture, psychology, behaviourism, story-telling, sound design and more. If the role of a transmedia producer is often likened to that of an orchestra conductor, then creating VR could be compared to the work of a magician, gathering techniques to guide the viewer towards creating an experience. Sleight of hand meets sleight of mind. The fact is that with VR, the stories are locked behind a device, requiring a sequence of steps by the viewer/user/player. The barriers to entry are high, which means the pay-offs should be more than worth the effort.

> "Anything can happen if you let it."
> *Mary Poppins*

The VR panel on policy will raise questions around external vs internal regulation and key factors for best practice. Whilst it may be early to discuss best practice, the industry runs the risk of being regulated from the outside, perhaps by those without the vision or experience to avoid choking off the creativity so desperately needed to assess the way forward. Our panel of researchers, child psychologists and story-tellers will discuss industry standards as well as the evidence and results of early testing with children, along with the short- and long-term physical side effects, content moderation and suitability of content.

It seems that the safety of VR varies by the type of content and time spent using it, as well as the considerations of each individual child. There are valid caution triggers around VR for children: immersion, addiction, cognitive overload and more, which may be solved by design structures such as duration, replayability and story-centric interaction. This could mean that VR headsets may be less of a problem than books or smartphones and it's possible that creative structure will play a significant role in the safe and optimum experience for

RESEARCH

children in VR.

> "This isn't flying. This is falling with style."
> Buzz Lightyear, *Toy Story*

Creatively, we need to continue testing and failing, fast. The VR creative session will bring to light existing work and best practices along with the challenges and possibilities of creating for this environment. When the content is device dependent, issues such as onboarding and acclimatization centre around design, and when you have children as young as eight recounting their VR experiences as if they really happened, it's worth looking at how to manage expectations and attempt to solve some of the concerns through thinking about design.

> "Giving up is for rookies."
> Philoctetes, *Hercules*

Of course, "show me the money" is what catapults any new form of entertainment and content creation from an indulgent hobby to a tangible proposal. The VR business session will look at the pipelines of business models for children's VR, from discoverability, marketing and onboarding to distribution and monetization, bringing experience from the gaming and app worlds. Without a business model behind VR, it loses both its glittering allure and its credibility.

The Way Forward

There is both excitement and fear around VR creating a strong sense of illusion and embodiment. As such, due diligence is paramount as we travel into this new frontier. There is a code of ethical conduct that comes with smart and responsive design thinking and the effects of long-term immersion and illusions of embodiment will help to determine best practices and avoid risky content.

Although it is developing at breakneck speed, technology still has some distance to go, and the role of AR/MR is perhaps more crucial in the short-to-medium term for both the consumer and corporate markets. What is clear is that VR/AR/MR are not just passing fads – over the next three to five years we will see these technologies appear in a broad variety of contexts, both inside and outside the home, with the potential to reshape entire industries.

We need to establish best practices: blending ethics, great design and immersive, engaging stories with robust business models. As cautious as many are about kids and VR, lots of us are rushing towards VR with excitement. I remain an excited sceptic, with a huge sense of responsibility to create safe and engaging story experiences for children (and adults), convinced that design can alleviate many of the concerns, coupled with story experiences that under-promise and over-deliver.

> "If you walk the footsteps of a stranger, you'll learn things you never knew."
> *Pocahontas*

CAN YOU GROW AN OPEN MIND THROUGH PLAY?

REBECCA ATKINSON

2016 was a big year for diversity in the toy box. Lego issued the world's first mini-figure with a wheelchair and disabled characters were included for the first time in the Lego Dimensions computer game, *Fantastic Beasts and Where to Find Them*. Playmobil is also said to be developing a line of disabled characters following a change.org petition signed by over 50,000 people, and Lottie.com dolls will be releasing a doll with a cochlear implant in response to the viral #ToyLikeMe campaign later this year.

Until now, the toy industry has perhaps made the assumption that disabled toys are for disabled children, therefore representing a niche market. This would certainly explain the dearth of representation in the toy box to date.

Research has found that disabled children are at an increased risk of low self-esteem. Tom Shakespeare, Professor of Disability Research at the University of East Anglia, explains that "low self-esteem can occur because of the reactions these children face in daily life and the lack of positive role models in our culture. If they never see themselves in stories, films, toys, then they may feel like permanent outsiders in the world."

When a disabled child sees themselves represented in mainstream toys and media, they see that they matter, that they are important in society and are part of the fun and games, which increases self-esteem and has a positive effect on development. But is it possible that there are further benefits? Can disabled toys help to open the minds of non-disabled children?

David and Victoria Beckham's daughter Harper

RESEARCH

Images from #ToyLikeMe photography exhibition Toy Box Tales, currently touring UK hospitals.

was pictured in August 2016 carrying a toy wheelchair through LA airport, prompting the *Daily Mail*'s Sarah Vine to write a column entitled "Is it healthy to give a child a disability doll?". Dr Sian Jones, a psychologist and academic at Goldsmiths, University of London, has been asking the same question in a research project conducted at London's Science Museum. Dr Jones looked at the attitudes of non-disabled children to their disabled peers before and after playing with disability representative toys.

"There was a positive effect on interactions," she said in a BBC interview. "We measured children's intentions to make friends before and after they'd played with disabled characters and we found that children were more willing to make friends with a child with a disability after playing with a wheelchair-using toy."

The study, which involved hundreds of children, found attitudinal change after just three minutes of play, which Jones argues could be "profound, because it represents a cheap and easy intervention to combat prejudice."

Disabled children growing positive self-esteem and non-disabled children gaining open minds are solid arguments for increasing representation in the toy box, but how do you square this with the commercial demands of the market? If, as Dr Jones' research concludes, it's possible to educate generations of children to have a more open mind by playing with diverse toys, the market could far outstrip the perceived "niche" that is disabled children and their families. Every nursery, childcare setting and primary school in the world could present as a consumer.

facebook.com/toylikeme
Twitter: @toylikeme

RETHINKING TODDLERS AND TV

CARY BAZALGETTE

"The cinema, under wise guidance, may be made a powerful influence for good; if neglected, if its abuse is unchecked, its potentialities for evil are manifold."

The Cinema: Its Present Position and Future Possibilities, p. xxi
National Council for Public Morals (NCPM), 1917

Try an online search for "toddlers and TV". The results will indicate that attitudes to screen entertainment for children haven't changed much in 100 years, since the above NCPM pronouncement. Many of your search results will veer towards "potentialities for evil", citing obesity, brain damage, ADHD syndrome and the like; others will favour the "influence for good" end of the spectrum, asserting that children learn things from TV that help their language development and "school readiness", or that it gives parents a break and it's harmless fun.

I'll come clean and confess that I haven't actually analysed all the 34,300,000+ results that Google gave when I tried this search, but I am prepared to bet that virtually all of them lay somewhere on this "risks and benefits" spectrum. It frames not only a social media discussion of children and TV, but also academic research on the topic – at least in Anglophone countries. It has now extended beyond TV to include a wide range of cultural forms and practices, which all get lumped together under technological terms like "screen" or "digital" and are assumed to present risks and/or benefits to children.

We thus have an agenda that is stifling proper discussion

about the specificities of these different forms and practices, about the varying quality of content, and how children engage with it. It is an agenda that is demeaning to children, framing them either as victims or beneficiaries, while neglecting their achievements in figuring out how to understand a wide range of densely multimodal media. Learning how to play *Toca Dance* on a smartphone, and learning how to make sense of, say, *Uncle Grandpa* (Cartoon Network) each demand complex – and very different – sets of skills, most of which children learn by the age of four. Just because this learning happens early doesn't mean it is simple, or not worth investigating.

I am interested in how two-year-olds learn to make sense of moving-image media. Two-year-olds are not studied as much as infants, pre-schoolers or schoolchildren. They are harder to access (they can't be reached through clinics or nurseries) and when you do get access to them, they don't sit in one place ready to be observed. But the third year of life is an amazing period in terms of the learning trajectories that dramatically accelerate: verbal language, imaginative play, a sense of personal identity, empathy with others, physical dexterity, symbolic forms such as letters and numbers, narratives, jokes – and, I would argue, how to make sense of films.

As many scholars have admitted, the only way to overcome the difficulties of studying two-year-olds is to do it in the home. Like some significant predecessors (Darwin, Piaget), I studied my own family: my twin grandchildren – a girl and a boy – for 20 months, starting when they were 22 months old. I observed and videoed their viewings of TV programmes and DVDs of short and feature-length films, accumulating 12 hours of video and reams of observation notes.

The first thing I noticed was their intense attention to the material that interested them. Seven minutes standing perfectly still, bracing herself against the nearest bit of furniture to maintain her balance, is a remarkable thing for a 22-month-old to decide to do. The twins had definite, individual preferences about what they wanted to watch and what to attend to, often standing close to the screen and occasionally touching it in a delicate, exploratory way, either with a finger or with the flat of the hand. Frowns, deeper breathing and pursed lips would indicate heightened attention and sometimes apprehension.

You could interpret this behaviour as evidence of distress, anxiety or incomprehension if you were viewing it through a "risk" lens; I was not. In any case, I knew these children well, and they were in a familiar environment – factors that, I argue, are essential for understanding two-year-olds' everyday activities. The twins *were* sometimes frightened or apprehensive. For example, when she was just two, Connie was extremely upset by a rope-breaking incident in *Peppa Pig: Sports Day* – not a programme likely to be high on anyone's child-protection agenda. But her response indicated that she was engaged with the narrative arc of the programme.

From analysing my video material, I am confident that the children's focused attention was driven by what the neuroscientist Jaak Panksepp has called the "seeking" emotion. He characterizes this in terms of excitement, anticipation and investigation, seeing it as the emotion that "gradually helps cement the perception of causal connections in the world and thereby creates ideas"(Panksepp 2004, p. 50).

I have used embodied cognition theory, with its links to neuroscience and evolutionary biology, in examining the fine detail of the children's volatile, emotionally expressive behaviour around the TV screen. I found it particularly significant that their most intensely attentive moments were when they were presented with material that was, for them, new and unusual in some way. Either or both of them might demand to see it again, and then be equally attentive to subsequent viewings, but would indicate with exclamations and gestures when they remembered what was coming next and recognized characters or props.

Wanting to see certain films or programmes repeatedly is a well-known phenomenon with toddler viewers, but one that has not been addressed much by researchers. We tend to use the language of affect in describing toddlers' love of re-viewing, i.e. "he just *loves Baby Jake*" or "*In the Night Garden* used to be her favourite, until she got bored with it". But in my discussions about the project with my daughter, she invented the term "used up" to describe the children's transferences of film loyalties: "they suck all they can out of it", she would say.

Watching my videos together with the twins' parents, we agreed that attentiveness and re-viewing were signs of a self-directed learning process, which included very distinct preferences about what they wanted to re-view and what they rejected as of no interest. The criteria that drove their preferences were difficult to identify, but it did seem that their interest was most often engaged by material that was at the edge of their capacity to make sense of it. This echoes Lev Vygotsky's comment on children's play and its concomitant learning: "in play a child always behaves beyond his average age, above his daily behaviour" (Vygotsky 1978, p. 102).

The social context was another vital element of the children's viewing experiences. Obviously I was always present when I was observing or videoing, but usually at least one other adult family member was there too. Either or both children might be sitting on someone's lap, or excitedly sharing pleasurable moments such as anticipating what was to come, identifying characters, enacting familiar routines with their mother, like shouting out what the very hungry caterpillar was going to eat next. They occupied an aural environment that included not only the soundtrack but also the utterances of other family members: comments, laughter, and emotive sounds like "ooh!" and "aha!" This was part of their growing awareness of the family's cultural practices, of which watching TV together was an important element. However, this did not mean that they always accepted adults' choices about what they might want to watch.

But what were they learning? On one level they were getting used to the basic "grammar" of the moving image, for example changes of scale from wide shots to close-ups; eyeline matches; non-diegetic sound. Paul Messaris argues that many filmic devices (such as a cutaway following an off-screen gaze) are easy to learn because they mimic instinctive human behaviour (Messaris 1994); jump-cuts and other devices for the management of time in narration are a little harder to learn.

The twins became interested in modality

judgments (see Hodge and Tripp 1986, Chapter 4), i.e. considering whether the presenter who says "see you tomorrow" really means it, and which bits of a scene mixing animation with live action are "real" and "pretend". Alfie developed a fear of endings and became extremely adept at recognizing the signs of an impending conclusion, even when he was not fully following the narrative. They became able to re-tell fragments of narrative, but I speculate that their grasp of narrative formats such as quests, tricks and magical transformations was well ahead of their capacity to express them verbally.

Understanding other people's intentions and goals is an essential part of understanding narrative, but it could also be the result of "selection during human evolution for powerful skills of intention-reading as well as for motivation to share psychological states with others" and therefore something that infants and toddlers can do (Tomasello et al. 2005, p. 690). This argument is strengthened by the discovery of mirror neurons: structures in the brains of primates and humans that motivate us to mimic, or at least empathize with, the actions of others. Contradicting the Cartesian separation of body and mind, this suggests that our capacity to "map others' … emotions and sensations onto our own viscero-motor and somatosensory systems" (Wojciehowski and Gallese 2011) is part of instinctive, early behaviour. It could thus be not only an important part of how toddlers make sense of TV, but a powerful argument for the importance of TV to toddlers.

A sample of two children, studied by an inevitably partial grandmother, could easily be dismissed as trivial stuff. But parenting sites on social media are full of observations like mine: intense attention, repeat viewing, finite phases of interest, joyful co-viewing with family members. Usually these are couched in "risk-benefit" terms, e.g. "… so it must be good for them really". Of course, most producers of children's TV believe in their hearts that their work is more important than that: they know that "being part of culture is a need human beings are born with – that culture, whatever its contents, is a natural function" (Trevarthen 1995, p. 5) and that films are part of our culture. So, I think that the industry should worry less about making a case for the educational value of children's TV, and instead speak from the heart.

References

Hodge, B. & D. Tripp. 1986. *Children and Television: A Semiotic Approach.* Cambridge: Polity Press.

Messaris, P. 1994. *Visual Literacy: Image, Mind and Reality.* Oxford: Westview Press.

Panksepp, J. 2004. *Affective Neuroscience.* Oxford: Oxford University Press.

Tomasello, M., M. Carpenter, J. Call, T. Behne & H. Moll (2005) Understanding and sharing intentions: The origins of cultural cognition. *Behavioral and Brain Sciences,* 28, 675-735.

Trevarthen, C. (1995) The Child's Need to Learn a Culture. *Children and Society,* 9, 5-19.

Vygotsky, L. 1978. *Mind in Society: The Development of Higher Psychological Processes.* Cambridge, Mass.: Harvard University Press.

Wojciehowski, H. C. & V. Gallese (2011) How Stories make us feel: Toward an Embodied Narratology. *California Italian Studies* 2.

FAKE NEWS

DR BECKY PARRY

Media studies, a subject designed to develop children's criticality, has generally been mocked in the UK for years now. The news media and politicians, in particular, have termed it a "mickey mouse" subject, eroding its value in schools. So much for developing children's skills to discern, make judgements and evaluate the veracity of the news. As a former media educator, I must be forgiven for my rueful raised eyebrow when calls are made about teaching children to recognize "fake news". This outcry or Twitter-storm was prompted because of the emergence of parody news on social media – so forgive me if I think someone, somewhere is missing the joke.

Trump may have stolen the term, but his redirection at the big news agencies in the US reminds us that all news is constructed and there are always "alternative facts". It is certainly hard to imagine a time when the need to develop public criticality was more urgent. Therefore, it seems timely to share an account of a research project in which children aged eight and nine undertook a programme of study about news. The story begins in a classroom in the east of England on a very wintery day. The children had begun to gather their own news for a local radio broadcast, a simulated news production activity common to media education in primary schools.

"A long time ago in a galaxy far, far away…" A whoop of excitement travels around the class like wild fire. The teacher has just shown his class a photo of a UFO which was "seen" by another staff member the night before. The photo is fictional as is the sighting – it's part of a simulated news production activity. The children are on their second day of producing a news programme and their excitement is not generated by the idea that a teacher has seen a UFO, nor is it disbelief; they are excited because one child has just worked out that they can use the story as news. Throughout the room the children's voices announce: "it's news", "we can use it as news". They look for confirmation from their teacher who affirms it, and they cheer.

This memorable moment took place during the Economic and Social Research Council-funded "Developing Media Literacy" research project led by the Institute of Education UCL, which focused on learning progression in media education. Working with two specialist media arts schools in the UK and their feeder primary schools, we undertook a sequence of learning activities in collaboration with teachers that enabled us to teach key media studies concepts, right across the age range. It is often assumed these sorts of experiences are superficial and don't reflect what really happens in the news-room. However, internationally, media educators recognize the increasing need for media or digital literacy which enables young people to navigate what Henry Jenkins (2006) describes as the "new global participatory culture". In this activity, focused on news, we aimed to confront what Jenkins calls the ethics challenge, that is to say:

The Participation Gap
The unequal access to the opportunities, experiences, skills, and knowledge that will prepare youth for full participation in the world of tomorrow

The Transparency Problem
The challenges young people face in learning to see clearly the ways that media shape perceptions of the world

The Ethics Challenge
The breakdown of traditional forms of professional training and socialization that might prepare young people for their increasingly public roles as media makers and community participants

(Jenkins 2006 p. 3)

During this week of news production simulation, the children took on the roles of reporters as well as accountants, advertisers and regulators. A cost was attached to all activities – resources (laptops, stationery), training and going out to do interviews all involved the children spending "money". The task was to produce a radio news bulletin for their target audience and to make a profit and beat their competitor groups. This may seem an unnecessarily complex simulation for a primary class, but it enabled the children to occupy roles well outside their own experience. In doing so, they encountered a series of ethical dilemmas and had to make what Jenkins describes as "Judgement – the ability to evaluate the reliability and credibility of different information sources". They also had to learn to engage with "Simulation – the ability to interpret and construct dynamic models of the real-world". (Jenkins 2006 p. 4). They had to balance the pursuit of truth and accuracy with an economic imperative and they had a strict deadline.

In their roles as news gatherers encountering the UFO story, the children were excited by what they recognized as a bigger item than those they had come up with so far which either copied national news or resembled a school newsletter. At this point they did not worry about the veracity of the story – they had a strong ability to suspend disbelief. However, they were also developing an explicit understanding of magnitude as a criteria for news gathering, experiencing "in role" the same feeling a journalist might have when a "big" story breaks.

Later in the process, I talked to Matthew who was upset. Having been checked by the two "regulators", the news story he had written was found to be inaccurate. He had covered a story about a child who had fallen in the icy conditions outside and rather than interview the child and find out what had happened, he had decided to just "make it up". It's my guess that Matthew didn't think it was that important and, what's more, he knew there was a cost involved to a face to face interview.

However, he hadn't bargained on the seriousness with which the "regulators" took their role of fact checking. They interviewed the child and were in possession of the "facts", quickly realizing Matthews's account didn't match up. Later, Matthew reflected that "you shouldn't lie" and fellow group member Isaac added, "well if it's just about how many pieces a chocolate bar broke into it doesn't matter, but if it is like the world is going to blow up, it does". Matthew got to rewrite his story but his group had to pay a hefty fine. What bothered him was the thought that his group might not win and that his peers were disappointed he had lied.

The process of production created moments of crisis or decision-making which enabled the children to grapple with some of the most challenging issues we face in contemporary society. After Matthew had been fined, the children all began rapidly checking their sources of information. The authenticity of the UFO story was called into question and many of them dropped it for fear of being fined. Others decided to go ahead because, although it was clearly fake, it was something the *teachers* had made up – so that was OK! This programme of activity was key to our finding, that young children are capable of grappling with complex and abstract ethical issues, given the opportunity and a particular pedagogic approach.

Interestingly, the whole activity ran parallel to the aftermath of the Leveson Inquiry. When I interviewed the children later in the term, it was clear they had been paying attention to the news coverage, raising questions about the moral judgements of journalists listening to people's mobile phone messages.

Since this research project was reported, all traces of media education are long gone from the primary curriculum in England. Perhaps criticality is surplus to requirements in our post-truth, fake news times; it hardly serves those seeking political office or positions of power. In contrast, media education in Finland is advanced, with children studying news from the earliest age and the government funding the production of media education resources, including, for example, the rather wonderful "populism bingo". Given the absence of media education in schools in the UK, perhaps it is the children's media industry, with its commitment to young audiences, who can begin to produce content which nurtures the skills children need to represent their own truths ethically and with judgement. It's a challenge worth confronting.

Jenkins, H. (2006). White Paper: Confronting the Challenges of Participatory Culture: Media Education for the 21st Century. *Berkeley, US: MacArthur Foundation.*

COMING OF AGE ONLINE: THE CASE FOR YOUTH-LED DIGITAL RESILIENCE

SAM LAWYER AND YARA FARRAN

There are currently a range of terms used to describe how young people can navigate opportunities and risks online. "Digital literacy", "e-skills", "online self-efficacy" and "resilience" are among the advised toolkit allowing children to benefit from digital technology while avoiding or coping with associated harms. Such language is now widely cited among media institutions, educators, parents and children alike, but a singular definition continues to evade these communities and questions remain about how children incorporate these skills into their everyday media practices. We spoke with some of the leading UK academics researching young people and digital technology to get their take on how these terms have evolved, and how children conceive the possibilities and challenges of the internet.

Although this is a topic affecting people of all ages, there are several reasons why young people have been particularly apt subjects for academic research in this area. Dr Sonia Livingstone OBE, Professor of Social Psychology at the London School of Economics, notes that kids are in constant "learning mode" as they manage new experiences and set life goals. Combining this outlook with the digital environment they were born into, we see a focus on networks, keenness to innovate and an openness to "just-in-time learning". Due to age, kids may also experience higher levels of adversity, amplified because they are "less experienced in the ways of the world" and more vulnerable to societal pressures, which society in turn has a responsibility to protect them from.

Over the last decade, academia has built the foundation for literature on online risk from what used to be a very limited pool of resources. Dr Leslie Haddon, a senior researcher at the London School of Economics and co-author of *EU Kids Online* (2014), says that today "there are fewer and fewer areas that haven't been explored" in terms of online safety, and that researchers are "now at the stage of arguing over details". Qualitative research such as Dr Haddon's is particularly useful in refining our understanding of the online experiences of young people, and in challenging assumptions built into earlier survey data. Thankfully, Dr Haddon notes that the most serious risks online are also the least occurring, and the low incidence rates often become clearer through understanding "what's happening behind these statistics".

Such research has also been incorporated into the teaching of parents and educators, who warmly welcome empirical evidence on this topic. Dr Haddon notes that because of the array of publications and online forums offering differing advice on parenting in the digital age, "there's a lot of puzzlement" and it can be "really quite problematic to know what to do". Most parents he meets are trying their best to educate themselves and their children on the appropriate skills and safety practices, and this is supplemented by the training their children are given at school. Dr Haddon cites one of the biggest indications of this as the institutionalized language used by young people in interviews. When describing their online experiences, they are clearly using terms they've been taught to incorporate into their internet vocabulary.

Young people are responsive to this digital literacy training, but they also tend to have more positive perceptions of online opportunities and apply critical thinking to such advice. In Dr Livingstone's research, children most often list "communication, networking, identity exploration and information" as the key opportunities of digital engagement, with bullying, harmful content (e.g. violence, pornography, humiliating content, reputational threats) and loss of privacy as the risks. Considering such risks, Dr Haddon finds that across age groups, young people feel that the internet has positively affected their lives; they see exciting experiences where adults may see threats. One example he gives is the long-held worry of "stranger danger" – many children perceive meeting new people online as a fun and exciting experience. He explains that warnings about talking to strangers online will not always deter young people, since "occasionally they'll do it and it's quite pleasant. They've got their own strategies for dealing with it" and "they're not taking this blanket advice". As with any type of formalized training, young people are able to extract from it what they need, and develop their own strategies for those times when their interests fall outside of the framework.

Professor of Educational Technology at Newcastle University, Sugata Mitra, agrees that young people online "seem far less concerned with risks than we are" and emphasizes the need to support children as agents capable of self-directed learning. In his view, the term "digital resilience" is really "more for corporates or adults than for children", which is problematic because it favours knowledge systems created by adults and corporations as opposed to those fashioned by young people. Adult knowledge systems tend to be prescriptive in teaching youth about what is "good' and "bad", thus possibly undermining the ability of young people to draw these conclusions themselves. His research suggests that peer-to-peer education fosters collective engagement, and affirms the need for adults to create spaces for children to explore safety and risk on their own terms. Within this pro-youth model, the development of digital resilience becomes a transformative exercise of agency and power through which young people can focus on both individual and collective learning.

Aside from the educational and affective benefits provided by peer-to-peer learning in this context, young people may also play a key part in helping us understand how to optimize digital literacy as a broader society. As Dr Livingstone says, "we're in the middle of a huge social experiment, but we can't assign people to digital and non-digital lives, to compare the differences [or] wait twenty years to see how people grow up in the digital age and then go back and change things". Amid the challenging task of identifying which people are most resilient on the internet and why, young people can inform us in highly pragmatic ways. Dr Livingstone asserts that young people "could play greater roles in the development of public policy, industry innovation and educational practice, if they were only consulted, listened to and engaged with more substantially and in all their diversity". Examining young people and digital resilience is an exercise that has considerable benefits across a variety of sectors, and the first step in realizing this is to acknowledge the unique value in their ideas and experiences.

The research of Dr Livingstone, Dr Haddon and Professor Mitra strongly supports the idea that the perspectives of young people should be at the forefront of conversations about resilience online. In intentionally developing peer-to-peer initiatives, digital resilience can shift from being an institutional endeavour to one that is collaborative and liberating for media practitioners, researchers, parents and youth alike. As members of the children's media community, it is imperative that we now reflect on our own perspectives and practices, and make space for youth-led digital resiliency in all that we do.

FROM SCREEN TO PAGE: CHILDREN'S MEDIA IN THEIR WRITING

LUCY TAYLOR

We know that children are proficient users of a wide range of media. They access, interact with, play with and consume visual, audio and written texts. Children can watch film and television programmes designed especially for them, along with stories, poems, comics, newspapers and more. They can play a variety of games on digital devices in which they might take the form of an avatar, build and destroy worlds, encounter other creatures, other players and other selves. Children also engage with online content, which may or may not be designed with a child audience in mind, following favoured YouTubers and vloggers, watching and learning as games are played, music is performed or items are "unboxed". Indeed, Ofcom (2016), report that YouTube is the preferred content destination for children aged 8–15, with younger children preferring "TV-like" content and older children choosing "music videos, game tutorials and joke or prank videos". [1]

---
1   Ofcom (2016) Children and parents: media use and attitudes report

It should not be surprising, then, that the variety of media influences experienced by children is reflected in their own writing. In a research project exploring children's independent writing, I worked with two classes of year 5 children (aged 9–10). Participants were given a free choice writing journal in which they were asked to write whatever they enjoyed writing over the period of half a school term. Some were very prolific and required additional journals; others wrote very little. However, in general, the children chose to write in a remarkable range of genres and styles, including narrative, prose non-fiction, poetry, labelled illustrations, comics, lists, personal accounts and songs.

The writing often included clear references to films, television or computer games with which they were familiar. Children wrote stories about Mr Bean, Disney characters, characters from *Goosebumps* and from "Five Nights at Freddy's" (a jump-scare computer game). There were also references to popular characters from books and films, such as Greg from *Diary of a Wimpy Kid*[2] and Harry Potter.

Their fiction writing contained references to game shows and contests, and

---
2   Jeff Kinney, Diary of a Wimpy Kid series (Puffin)

RESEARCH

Figure 1

the children were very clear that they saw the media they encountered as a potential resource to draw on. One writer, Adnan, whose dinosaur story included a time travel clock, told me that he "got it on TV, on CBeebies" and another, Jake, acknowledged that "it felt like I was watching the story while I was writing it". Children were creative in their responses: one child wrote an acrostic poem using the letters of the internet meme "Nyan Cat" and others wrote comics which featured a Pokémon version of *The Hunger Games*. It's important to say that the children drew on the styles and content of favourite texts, not copying but imitating and transforming in imaginative ways. One of the most fascinating aspects of their writing was the way in which they were able to transform one media into another.

A particularly interesting example of this was "Andy", whose Pokémon comics were a written hybrid of the different media in which Pokémon can be played. Pokémon can be played as a trading card game; in a series of video games featuring adventures, role-play, strategy, and puzzles and in the much-hyped *Pokémon GO* which involves hunting virtual Pokémon, via an app, in real places. Pokémon adventures can also be read in print or online in comic strip form.

Figure 1 shows the first two panels of a comic strip written by Andy. In the first panel he introduces the protagonist who is engaged in a game, perhaps *Pokémon GO,* indicated by his speech "Oh wow a wild Weedle!", but is also a character in the narrative.

Andy has created a setting for the action with stylized trees shown at an angle in a manner reminiscent of the dynamic visual representations seen in Manga comics. The carefully delineated double lined edges for the panels suggest a comic book style. However, in the second panel Andy moves very clearly into the online world. There is a battle between the wild Weedle and Pikachu. The panel shows the "health bar" for each character, the Weedle's in the top right and Pikachu's in the bottom left. Speech bubbles show these words of encouragement, presumably called by the protagonist from panel 1: "Go Pikachu!, Use thunderbolt!" and the information on the screen tells us that "Weedle used Struggle". Struggle and thunderbolt are weapons that can be deployed in a fight; the thunderbolt is shown being directed by Pikachu towards the Weedle.

This panel creates a hybrid of the video game experience, represented by the stylized fight scene, and the comic strip experience, where a protagonist

CHILDREN'S MEDIA YEARBOOK 2017

Figure 2

participates in the events of the narrative through speech bubbles. A similar combination of the comic strip and video game experience can be seen in Figure 2, taken from further on in the same piece of writing.

The style and organization of the panels is particularly interesting. Under the title "Later the next day", Andy has divided the page into two panels, divided by a diagonal line leaning to the right. In the left-hand panel, the protagonist kneels in front of a dark cave or tunnel entrance and asks, "Hey Pikachu, what's in there?" Pikachu also looks into the cave, with his back to the reader, and gives the reply "Pika", his characteristic sound. In the right-hand panel, Pikachu has entered the tunnel, cleverly placed by Andy on the line between the two panels so that both the character and the reader have to pass through to reach the next panel. Andy further demonstrates his skills in multimodal communication by showing the fearful response of Pikachu on the character's face, not in the words which again only say "Pika!"

There is a door which Pikachu has to pass through, but before it are a number of obstacles hanging from the ceiling, which may be bats or another kind of enemy creature. Andy gives no explanation, he makes the assumption that a reader familiar with the conventions of adventure video games will know that where there is a door it should be reached and opened, and where there are obstacles they should be avoided. Below these two panels is a long thin panel stretching all the way across the page.

Pikachu is shown at the left of the page ready to embark on an attempt to reach the door whilst avoiding the hanging obstacles, his bouncing motion indicated in the wavy line on the floor. Again, this panel is much more closely aligned to video game imagery and experience than it is to the features of written comics. In the panel on the bottom left, Pikachu arrives triumphantly and opens the door, his smiling face and the large, upper case "PIKA!" indicating success. The adventure then continues in the next panel, in the room which Pikachu has just gained access to.

In creating this piece, Andy has made some significant decisions as the author. In choosing to write in a comic form in the first place, he is acknowledging that the best way to tell the story he wants to tell, or to represent the experience he wants to represent, is to use a form which makes use of text and image. The subject matter he has chosen, that of a Pokémon adventure, needs to be expressed in both visual and textual ways. He chooses a multimodal approach but goes on to adapt and transform his written text by making use of the affordances of the different media he has interacted with.

Where the visual features of video games are more appropriate he makes use of them in his text, and it's the same in instances where those of the comic are more useful. Andy's experiences with a variety of media mean that he is well placed to draw on a variety of visual, textual and narrative styles to create something new, taking the reader of a printed text into the world of a video game.

Andy's skills as a writer of this type of text may not be appreciated or called upon in the primary classroom, but he is clearly well placed to take and make meaning from a range of evolving media. The invitation to write freely, provided by the research project, enabled Andy and his classmates to draw on personal experiences with different media. Their writing was quite different to that required of them by the school curriculum, but it showed creativity and skill. Children are capable of taking and making meaning from the range of media they encounter and they see it as a resource to use in their own writing and other forms of creative work.

The range and variety of children's writing in this project suggest that

- Children's media continues to play an important role in their shared cultural experience
- Children's media is an important resource for children's own creativity, particularly their writing
- Given the opportunity, children are taking on the challenges of transforming media in their writing in creative and imaginative ways, from screen to page.

This research contributes to a wider body of research demonstrating that media production for children need not be driven by the requirements of the school curriculum. Those making media for children are modelling creativity and providing children with resources for their own writing. And, given the right opportunities, children are more than capable of responding playfully and imaginatively.

Suggestions for further reading:

Dyson, A. H. (2002). *The brothers and sisters learn to write: Popular literacies in childhood and school cultures* (Vol. 64). Teachers College Press.

Willett, R. (2005). 'Baddies' in the classroom: media education and narrative writing. *Literacy, 39*(3), 142-148.

Marsh, J. (2000). 'But I want to fly too!': Girls and superhero play in the infant classroom. *Gender and Education, 12*(2), 209-220.

Bearne, E. (2004). Multimodal texts. *Literacy moves on: Using popular culture, new technologies and critical literacy in the primary classroom,* 16.

"IT WASN'T REALLY ABOUT THE POKÉMON": PARENTS' PERSPECTIVES ON A LOCATION-BASED MOBILE GAME

KILEY SOBEL WITH ARPITA BHATTACHARYA, ALEXIS HINIKER, JIN HA LEE, PHD, JULIE A KIENTZ, PHD, AND JASON C YIP, PHD

On 6 July 2016, Niantic, Inc. released *Pokémon GO*, a location-based mobile game in which players use their device's location-tracking capabilities to navigate their avatar in the virtual world by *physically* moving through the real world to meaningful locations. (One of these locations is called a PokéStop and you can now filter results on Yelp.com by "PokéStop Nearby!") Through this gameplay based on the physical environment, players can locate, capture, battle, and train virtual characters called Pokémon, like Pikachu, Squirtle, and Jigglypuff.

Pokémon GO also has an optional augmented reality feature so that Pokémon appear on the screen as if actually located near you in the physical world (Jigglypuff just might be sitting next to you right now!). According to Niantic, *Pokémon GO* has been downloaded over 650 million times since its release, and while it might have seemed like the craze for the game could be over, on 7 April 2017 at Google Developer Day at the Game Developer Conference, Niantic announced that over 65 million people worldwide still play *Pokémon Go* each month.

RESEARCH

Screen time tensions and family co-engagement with technology

Immediately after *Pokémon GO*'s emergence, our research team at the University of Washington began seeing media articles about the game and familial tension, with parents mediating their children's screen time. Such articles claimed that *Pokémon GO* might be "the world's most dangerous game" but that it also facilitates family bonding. It was indeed difficult, in our community, not to notice the *extremely* large crowds of people in public spaces playing the game, including many families and people of all ages. It quickly became clear that parents and their children were not only playing *Pokémon GO* individually, but also together. And so, we began to wonder – beyond the on-boarding due to *Pokémon* itself (the franchise has been around since 1996, meaning that many of today's parents played Pokémon when they were children) – what was going on that was leading parents to allow their children to play, both solo and as a family?

We surmised that location-based games like this can change the way we think about screen time. There is often a fear that too much time with screens is displacing "healthier", more "educational" and more "social" activities. However, *Pokémon GO* might provide a case to show that engagement with technology can, in fact, be active, educational, and social.

This is important because, as the Joan Ganz Cooney Center and LIFE Center have taught us, jointly engaging with new media is beneficial for children; it leads to the creation of meaningful connections among representations, interests, and experiences. Joint media engagement (JME) includes viewing, playing, searching, reading, contributing, and creating with either digital or traditional media.

So, due to the global phenomenon of *Pokémon GO*, we were given a window into parental attitudes towards (and family experiences with) technology on a large scale, which we as a research community have never been able to study before.

Research

In our research, we asked: what are the experiences, perspectives and attitudes of parents regarding their children playing location-based mobile games? We wanted to learn more about three main topics:

- The choices parents and families make on how to play the game
- Rules set by parents about their children's game use and why
- How parents might jointly engage in this type of gaming with their children

To answer these questions, we administered a qualitative survey to 67 parents (the majority from the U.S.) and conducted interviews with 20 parents in Seattle, Washington from late-July to mid-August 2016. We approached and interviewed all 20 interview participants in a large public space like Bellevue Downtown Park just outside of Seattle, where parents were playing with their children or watching their children play *Pokémon GO*. Finding participants was not at all difficult. However, running with families to catch Charmander or Dratini during the interview was something we hadn't experienced in previous research projects!

Findings

Other than catching a great variety of Pokémon, what did we find out? In addition to exercise and time outdoors, parents valued the fact that play encouraged family bonding. Playing together brought families closer, strengthening common interests and sometimes transcending beyond the game itself. *Pokémon GO* became something a mum was able to talk to her usually not-so-talkative son about and something that made a daughter feel excited to hang out with her dad. Playing *Pokémon GO* also easily fit into families' lives, either coinciding with other activities like family dog walks or running errands, or becoming specifically planned family *Pokémon GO* time (which some families dubbed "Pokéwalks").

Here are a few of our favourite quotes from our participants:

> "I love that this is a game we can play together as a family, and I often play a little during the day (alone) so we can talk about my progress at night. My daughter's enthusiasm is turning me into a gamer!"
> 37-year-old mother with 7-year-old daughter

> "We were both running together [to catch a Pokémon], and she was looking at me, and she was smiling. It was just a great experience. It turned out it was a Cubone [a type of Pokémon]. I think that was her first Cubone, so that was cool. But it wasn't really about the Pokémon."
> 31-year-old father with 7-year-old daughter

> "We go out for long nightly walks as a family… We stop when we see Pokémon and they help to catch them. [The kids] get really excited to go out for walks, so I love taking them."
> 31-year-old mother with 3-year-old daughter and 1-year-old child

> "We came down [to the park] where lots of other moms came down with their kids. We all sat together… We could catch lots of stuff. We all took turns to go off … it was a really nice afternoon. It was the first time [my family] had a picnic in a couple years. It was because of *Pokémon GO*."
> 44-year-old father with 4-year-old and 7-year-old daughters

We found that while parents sometimes had traditional screen time concerns about gameplay, they also had new concerns about safety in real-world environments, including worrying about their children being harmed by strangers or getting hurt by not looking while walking. Parents made rules and gameplay choices centred around these new concerns to ensure their children were safe. For example, parents reported always accompanying their children and taking turns when playing, as well as staying in control of the mobile device during gameplay to make sure their children were not harmed.

RESEARCH

Takeaways

What can we, as designers, researchers, and parents, take away from this study? We hope it can help us begin to understand what makes *Pokémon GO* successful for joint engagement between parents and children, which can later aid in designing, studying, and co-playing these types of games with children.

Firstly, we believe that *Pokémon GO* was successful for productive joint media engagement because it supports the six conditions that help families and children come together with digital media:

- **Mutual engagement:** *Pokémon GO* lets people of all ages participate equally. Children and parents can take turns catching Pokémon, or children can throw balls in the game while parents evolve characters
- **Dialogic inquiry:** Family members asked each other questions, learned about characters together, and talked about the locations where they were playing
- **Co-creation:** Families can have shared experiences while playing *Pokémon GO*. In our research, parents and children learned about the game together and taught each other how to play
- **Boundary crossing:** The game appeals to players of multiple generations. Parents who had played Pokémon as kids enjoyed sharing the new game with their own children, who in turn were often pleased to be able to teach their parents about it
- **Intention to develop:** We found that all players were excited to level up. Parents and children alike played separately during the week and then shared their progress with one another
- **Focus on content, not control:** *Pokémon GO*'s simple game mechanics allow people of all ages to engage in play. Parents and children were able to share control, walk and interact with each other, and they did not have to rely on looking at the screen continuously to play.

Secondly, based on our research, there are other specific qualities about *Pokémon GO* that make it particularly encouraging for productive joint family media engagement. As a location-based mobile game, *Pokémon GO* hinges on players going outside, walking, learning about the neighbourhood, working in teams, and being social. Therefore, the game reconciles some of the issues parents have with screen time, fitting into the lives of families well.

Pokémon GO even facilitated families and children connecting and being social with other people outside of the family, sometimes in very large numbers. A 43-year-old mother of a 16-year-old daughter found that, "In general, other [*Pokémon GO*] players are quite nice and friendly." A mother of a 10-year-old boy explained that while playing one night, her son worked with other players, "They were a team. It was really nice, you know, to open up those channels of communication." However, this attitude conflicts with parental concerns about strangers, highlighting the importance of parental mediation of this type of screen time.

Additionally, while *Pokémon GO* was not designed explicitly for co-use on a single device, it is effectively being used as such. We both saw and heard about a lot of passing back and forth of one device between family members. A 42-year-old mother and her 6-year-old son got about five minutes each with one phone. Another 46-year-old mother who plays with her 7-year-old son said that they set a timer for five minutes each to ensure equal turns. Perhaps because the gameplay can be shared in many different ways, it was especially appealing to parents and children for joint media engagement. Some parents wanted to consistently play the game with (and without) their children. Other parents wanted to watch their children play and be their cheerleaders, and some wanted to help when their assistance was necessary. The fact that the roles were not prescriptive allowed different types of families to participate together.

Overall, perhaps it was the Pokémon themselves that initially on-boarded families to play, but the valuable experiences of and interactions within families existed and continued to exist beyond the actual content of the game. Ultimately, it wasn't really about Pokémon. It was about the special bond and memories that families were able to create through playing together, and the ways that gameplay challenged adults' more traditional concerns about children's technology use. Without these important elements, we think the game's popularity for families would not have been sustained. We hope this work will inspire new study and design for families' joint participation with new media!

This article is based on research completed by Kiley Sobel, Arpita Bhattacharya, Alexis Hiniker, Dr Jin Ha Lee, Dr Julie A. Kientz, and Dr Jason C. Yip, all from the University of Washington. This work has been accepted for publication at the 2017 ACM CHI Conference on Human Factors in Computing Systems (CHI 2017), a leading international conference on Human-Computer Interaction. The research publication can be accessed here: http://dl.acm.org/citation.cfm?id=3025453.3025761.

CALL FOR REGULATION – CHILDREN'S DATA IN PERSONALIZED BOOKS AND READING RESOURCES

DR NATALIA KUCIRKOVA

We live in an era where what you read is what you get, with personalized news services, ads and social media feeds attempting to narrow down the vast amounts of information available online. For adults, personalized reading comes under the banner of saving us time and providing us with only what we love. For children, the benefits often outlined include increasing motivation and pleasure in reading through personalized and adaptive learning.

Personalized books and personalized reading for young children range from basic personalization (where a child's name is inserted into a popular fairy tale) to sophisticated models of personalization allowing children to add their own drawings to the story, add voice-overs or replace the characters' names with their own (e.g. Mr Glue Stories[1]). Personalized books are offered as interactive digital books downloadable on touch screens (e.g. Put Me In The Story[2]) or as classic printed books (e.g. Lost My Name[3]). In addition to supporting children to read for pleasure, personalization can be used in adaptive algorithms for children learning to read, with texts matched to the child's reading level, language scores or genre preferences (see the iRead project[4]).

There are several positives to personalized reading experiences. In

---

[1] http://mrgluestories.com/

[2] http://www.putmeinthestory.com/put-me-in-the-story-free-ipad-app.html

[3] https://www.lostmy.name/

[4] https://iread-project.eu/

one study[5], for example, we found that children learn more new words from reading a personalized book than from a non-personalized one. However, given the rising popularity of personalized books in the children's market and the global role of personalization in reading, it is important to consider the potential risks and concerns of digital personalization in children's reading.

For personalized books and book recommendation systems (such as children's digital libraries or book finders), publishers and producers collect data not only including children's names, addresses, gender and skin colour, but also their engagement patterns with the reading content in their databases (in the case of digital library systems). Both pose risks relating to the storage, use and sharing of this personal data as well as potential commercialization through aggregate data.

The ESRC-funded project "Supporting early language development and interest in reading with digital personalized books"[6], focuses on personalization in children's reading for pleasure. The project is hosted by the UCL Institute of Education (IOE) and aims to investigate how the language development and reading experience of children can be enhanced through the use of data. As part of this aim, we have conducted some focus group interviews with UK children's app designers, book publishers, international researchers and representatives from children's literacy charities. The results of these interviews have been discussed on the LSE Digital Parenting platform[7] and will feed into a toolkit that establishes ethical standards for the design of children's personalized books.

At a meeting with key publishers and designers of children's products in March 2017, there was a strong consensus among the participants that there is an urgent need for regulations and policy concerning children's personalized (reading) products. As one designer commented, "Certainly there should be regulations around the security of data – what can be captured and how it can be stored – so that we make sure that everything that is personalized is stored very securely."

The key concerns that emerged from our focus group interviews centred on reduced possibilities for innovative design, the educational use of children's data and the risk of increased marketing for young consumers.

Security and privacy risks

Given that, currently, there are no official national guidelines regarding the amount, storage or sharing of data collected by publishers and producers of personalized books, parents and other caregivers must trust that individual companies will have the integrity not to misuse or misplace their family data. In conversation with a producer of personalized books, one participant remarked, "In talking to you I have to trust that in a way you are using the company's own ethical standards rather than anything external. Which does raise the risk."

---

5   http://journals.sagepub.com/doi/

6   https://www.ucl.ac.uk/ioe/departments-centres/departments/learning-and-leadership/personalised-stories/

7   http://blogs.lse.ac.uk/parenting4digitalfuture/

RESEARCH

Marketisation of childhood

The participants were clear about the risk of digital personalization – it does not relate to basic personalization models but those that collect aggregate data: "It's not about your photos but patterns of behaviour that predict what you will buy." Another designer–parent commented, "It's not inconceivable that a family's aggregated data could be shared and could personalize the experience for the consumer – the little consumer, the child."

Reduced design innovation

The lack of guidance not only poses risks, but also hampers the work of publishers and producers who are interested in the creative and innovative design of children's reading products. As one children's app producer explained, "I think the reason why the regulations are important is that a lot of ideas die because, for example, there is a lot of stuff that we will not be able to do – it has that fear level to it. It kills it straight out. So, when it comes to various aspects of data and how that data can be used, I certainly think we need some comprehensive regulation and thinking around that, extending what COPPA [Children's Online Privacy Protection Act] does and keeping it more comprehensive."

Reduced learning benefits for the child

If there was clear guidance, the data captured through children's use of book recommendation systems could be used in a more coordinated way to benefit stronger learning. For instance, if data on children's favourite books were shared between school and home, there could be a more meaningful dialogue about children's reading experiences. As yet, publishers might collect some such data but are not aware of the possibilities, as one of the participants (an app designer) admitted: "I'm not that sure about the data. I know we collect some data but I don't think it's at anywhere near as sophisticated a level as you are talking about. Yeah, I think it's an interesting point because we could be using the data more effectively to see what they are enjoying, what they are not enjoying."

A guiding document could facilitate home–school dialogue around personalized reading if it specified the security and standardization parameters for capturing and storing data at home and school: "So having some kind of standardization to tackle storage of data would be good." The desire to enhance the learning value of children's data is there but the knowledge on how to do it securely and safely is lacking: "If I'm gathering a lot of data from my children at home and that can be shared with school in a way that helps my children in their formal learning environment, that's fantastic. I would like to do that, I would like to know how it's done in a secure way."

We are currently exploring the possibilities for developing UK guidance on the use of children's data for personalized products together with the Children's Media Foundation and the All Party Parliamentary Group (APPG) on Children's Media and the Arts. If you would like to be part of these discussions, please contact me at n.kucirkova@ucl.ac.uk.

Kids Industries are very *proud* to continue *supporting* the *important* work of the Children's Media Foundation

We make brands stronger with award winning Insight, Strategy and Creative.

www.kidsindustries.com

in linkedin.com/company/kids-industries   ✉ hello@kidsindustries.com   🐦 @KidsIndustries

GENERAL CONTENT.

PROJECT HOPE

LUCY MURPHY

—

I have been proud to work in the children's media industry for over 25 years. In that time, there have been many changes in what, where and how kids watch their favourite shows. Channels have come and gone, top shows have burned bright and in some cases burned out, and new technologies have emerged that delight and open up creative opportunities I would never have dreamt of a quarter of a century ago. What hasn't changed, though, is the passion, drive and determination of the people who work in this industry. But it's not just a drive to succeed – what really characterizes colleagues I have worked alongside, many of whom I count as dear friends – is the love they have for the audience, the children around the world who watch the shows, read the books and play with the games and toys we craft.

It was at a Children's Media Conference dinner last July, with a group of international broadcasters, friends and colleagues from the kids' industry, that Project Hope was born. It was the summer of Brexit and the run-up to the US elections and coverage of the refugee crisis was constant. There was a rise in the reporting of hate crimes and a general sense of great change and uncertainty. BBC Children's Alison Stewart sat next to me at the dinner and as we reflected on the unsettling impact of these global events on us as adults, we asked ourselves a simple question: How on earth must kids be feeling? And, of course, a very quick follow-up question: What could we do about it?

The idea spread to colleagues around the room. What if we acted together? What if we were to do what we do best and create great content – content that would fly in the face of all the negativity and turmoil reported, instead offering hope to kids around

the world feeling anxious and fearful?

Alison and I took the seed of that idea and over the following months we worked on a structure to this plan. We decided to create a series of 12 high-quality short films centring on the themes of kindness, empathy and tolerance, plus a digital campaign and a legacy outreach project for kids aged 4 to 12.

Rather than Sky and the BBC taking ownership of the project, the idea is that broadcasters and media companies around the world will join to fund and create it and then, crucially, share it. Without worrying about the usual discussions on windows and rights, these 12 films will live on linear channels, VOD platforms, websites and online. By sharing, we will ensure that they are seen by as wide an audience as possible, and by using our global network of partners going live all at the same time, there is maximum opportunity for this message of hope and kindness to be heard around the world.

We're aiming for Project Hope to become the beginning of something: a movement that gives kids tools and foundations that they can build on themselves and empowers them to pass on the message of hope and kindness to others. It's a bold ambition – but the huge response we have had from the village of the kids' media industry so far indicates that the raising of this particular "child" will indeed be shared.

If you are interested in finding out more about this initiative, visit joinprojecthope@gmail.com

OPPORTUNITIES IN THE CHILDREN'S FILM INDUSTRY

TIM CLAGUE

An industry opportunity for the children's media sector

We recently made a children's feature film called *Who Killed Nelson Nutmeg?* This was privately financed, with no grants or broadcasters attached and no commission.

We are regulars at film markets, such as Cannes, so we have a different view on the children's film market than perhaps many other producers. We feel that the UK is potentially missing out on a profitable sector.

Here are a few reasons why we think there is a lot of opportunity for British writers and producers right now.

We need to think beyond TV

In the UK right now, there is a lot of industry focus on children's television, and rightly so. We should be proud of our TV output and do what we can to encourage and support as much high-quality programming as possible. But any growth in the children's media sector will have to come from other means. Children are ready to accept media from other outputs. Are we ready to make it?

To enable a new culture of UK family films, we think there needs to be a shift of focus and expectation regarding the realities of production as well as the financial returns. We're not necessarily talking

NELSON NUTMEG PICTURES

Hollywood numbers here, but the end result of *Nelson Nutmeg* proved to us that making a film was a worthwhile endeavour. Perhaps more importantly, we discovered a new audience base keen to see more films of this type. So, if we can make good features at a sensible budget with private equity, we are bringing new money to make films for a new audience. That is real growth.

British writing rules, OK

Our writing experience also appealed to the European producers we met in Cannes, for two reasons:

Screenwriting Craft

Producers told us that European writers tend to be slightly esoteric or artistic in their approach to writing. One producer remarked, "they can come up with some great general ideas but then they struggle to produce a script that is slick and entertaining." Consequently, European producers are very willing to work with UK writers whom they perceive as story experts and highly knowledgeable of their craft.

Language

A lot of European productions will dub an English version of their project to help increase their international sales. Scripts can easily be translated via a language agency but producers informed us that these translations were often dry, boring and lacking in wordplay or culturally relevant gags. What's required is a writer (or maybe a production company leading a team of writers) to lift the bland translations to a suitable level. Will the final product end up on a British TV channel or cinema? It may or it may not, and this uncertainty could be the reason why this work is passing us by. We are so busy focusing on our existing UK-based contacts that we miss these wider international opportunities.

A strong market in Europe

As a company who makes lower budget children's movies, we feel somewhat isolated in the UK. For example, our film was the only live-action British children's film at the 2015 BFI London Film Festival. There are very few people producing movies in

Britain for a younger audience and it can be all too easy to think that this situation is mirrored elsewhere across Europe. In fact, the opposite is true.

Germany, for instance, has a major family film tradition. New child-focused films are released on a regular basis, meaning it becomes a habit for families to go to the cinema together. Polish producers described children's movies as a major growth market, and the same is true for Scandinavia, too.

This dedicated European approach to the family film genre provides great inspiration but also a basis for a stronger UK market going forward. More immediately, it offers an opportunity to get involved in co-productions – now is a great time to reach out and collaborate.

The pros and cons of funding

Several countries actively support children's films in a similar manner to how the Children's Film Foundation used to operate here. In the UK, there is no special fund or provision for making features aimed at a younger audience. This is regrettable but has the positive side-effect of making us much more commercially minded and willing to explore other funding methods such as pre-sales and broadcaster acquisition. Meanwhile, some production companies in Europe have become slightly grant-reliant, as the only perceived option to getting finance. However, this is actually a good opportunity for us: such companies have access to funding whereas we can generate private investment or potentially utilize our broadcast contacts. Together this could result in some great films, but only if we choose to collaborate and start filming.

In conclusion

There is definite potential to make more films for children in the UK but only if we shift our mindset from simply looking at the broadcasters. We must reach out to new people across the world and be proactive. The business is there if we decide we want it. Yes, we may need to adjust our entrenched business models, but that's true of every industry.

Nelson Nutmeg Pictures is now scaling up to meet the obvious demand and necessity for family films. We're looking forward to making more kids' and family films, not just talking about it. Who wants to join us?

Find out more about the Nelson Nutmeg Pictures slate of film ideas at www.nelsonnutmegpictures.com

"HUMOUR IS VERY MUCH A SOCIAL, INTERPERSONAL ACT"

LAVERNE ANTROBUS

It's quite hard to put one's finger exactly on what makes us laugh, but having just spent a weekend with a four-year-old, I've been catapulted into a hilarious world. I watched and participated in endless silly jokes and it was heart-warming, exhausting and infectious, connecting a group whose ages ranged from 1 to 78. There was wonderment in the eyes of the youngest among us, and I too felt transported back to a time of carefree abandon.

It made me think about humour more broadly: where we find it and how much we need it to connect us in bleak times. It made me think about how closely humour can teeter on the edge and how important it is to have some way of navigating when it has perhaps gone too far.

There is a real art form to constructing a narrative that holds the attention of a young audience and makes them want more. I felt exhausted at the end of the day as I realized that keeping the jokes alive was harder than my day job. Presenters keeping their performances relevant so that the audience keeps laughing is a real craft.

Dick and Dom are giving the keynote speech at this year's event and their work as a double act continues to command rich descriptions of them as legends within the industry. Their longevity, for me, is down to a number of key reasons. They communicate their close working relationship to their audience, and they really show the joy they get from creating hilariously tricky situations in which comedic effect is pushed to its limits.

Their relationship is at the heart of why children are forever drawn into their performances. They are friends who have a unique understanding of each other which includes that essential ingredient: a shared sense of fun. They support each other to think about the most precarious aspects of a joke and bear the burden of seeing it through together. One imagines they have conversations that begin, "What do you think would happen if we did this?" and that once the anarchic act has been identified, "lived" and laughed about, they then work out the delicate path they will need to tread to reach the goal of execution!

Dick and Dom have a perceptive ability to push the boundaries of humour, ensuring that risk taking is at the heart of what they do. Viewers are persuaded to come with them on the journey and to share the agony of trying to achieve the impossible with a straight face. Once Dick and Dom start to tell the story, there is no going back for anyone. As the viewers, we are invited to laugh at the unacceptable, share the responsibility for execution and figuratively hold hands with them until the end.

Perhaps the most appealing aspect of the relationship and the performance is to see Dick and Dom allowing their child selves airtime. There is no pretence, just unbridled enjoyment of the anarchy that they create. It's all fully owned and consumed by them, which makes joining in so much fun.

Allowing our "inner child" to come to the surface is important – Dick and Dom give us a unique opportunity to grapple with the complex emotions we can feel when making fun of someone, providing some valuable lessons about putting ourselves in the other person's shoes. They remind us that the joke must include the person who is being teased for everyone to feel OK.

So, back to my weekend with the young children. It was fun to let our minds go to new places together, not to be constrained by rules and to share jokes. Above all, it was great to feel free to allow my inner child to play.

UNBOXING ... A TODDLER'S GLASS OF WINE?

NELLIE MCQUINN

Did you know that if you heat a knife with five blowtorches and cut into dry ice, it screams? That yellow play doh dries out the quickest of all the colours? Did you know that unboxing videos have audio levels twice as loud as other content, or that it takes three adults to remove Batman from a bath of jelly?

How does my CV look? Do I get the job? My skill set is certainly diverse. My team and I can shoot up to 30 videos in a day. We work with play doh, red-hot knives, sumo suits, pregnant superheroes – and that's all in an average week. We can tell you the *exact* ratio of glue to borax to make perfect slime, the lyrics to every nursery rhyme, and to top it off we can sing them all in eleven languages. What I can't tell you is the magic formula. What makes a fad? Why does a video go viral? How can a gaming channel have more views than *double* the earth's population, and why has unboxing captured the imagination of the world's junior psyche?

What is unboxing even about?!

The Oxford English dictionary defines unboxing as:

> "An act or instance of removing a newly purchased product from its packaging and examining its features, typically when filmed and shared on a social media site."

Let's ignore for a moment the fact that this absurd phenomenon has made it into the Oxford English dictionary in the first place. Unboxing … is it an act? These children aren't experiencing the reality they're engrossed in. They can't feel the cardboard. There are no paper cuts, no frustration at those annoying little cable ties that stand between you and your final goal. Surely that, by definition, makes it an act; a piece of theatre, drama, or fiction. Say what you like about unboxing, it's capturing the attention of every chubby-faced toddler gripping a smudged, grubby iPad.

Unboxing represents the excitement of every Christmas morning and birthday party. Your child might not be ripping open the packaging or touching the toy, but that doesn't mean they aren't physically altered in the viewing process. The anticipation whilst waiting for the moment of unboxing increases adrenaline and endorphins in the brain.

There is physical change. This increased adrenaline causes air passages to dilate, blood vessels to contract as they redirect blood toward major muscle groups, a noticeable increase in strength and performance, and heightened levels of awareness. The rush of adrenaline can lead to addiction. Perhaps this is why the return rate on these channels and videos is so high.

The sound of an unboxing video is akin to the autonomous sensory meridian response (ASMR) videos that are also taking the internet by storm. The unboxing videos my company creates are significantly more successful with live audio (we have experimented doing unboxing videos using only music – they didn't catch). From a production perspective, the sound is far louder than any other content we create and the volume would be considered poor post-production technique in any other style of content. A quick Wikipedia search on ASMR claims that the feeling of watching these videos is "akin to the feeling of a mild electrical current… or the carbonated bubbles in a glass of champagne". Perhaps unboxing videos are a toddler's way of unwinding after a tough day in the sandbox, the same way an adult has a glass of wine after work. How innocent are these videos? Are we actually creating a new generation of addicts?

The unboxing marketplace is now saturated. Fun Toys Collector (formerly of DC Toys Collector fame) has dominated the charts for several years now and it feels as if this fad is winding up. Multi-channel networks are looking forward. What's next? What seemingly innocent, yet hard core addiction can we inflict upon the next generation of touchscreen tethered tots?

Perhaps this time next year at CMC we will have the answer. We will all have cracked the elusive code of what it means to catch a trend, go viral and generate huge success in the process. Then again, perhaps we will be none the wiser and a new trend/platform/production will have surprised us all. At that point, I'll be sneaking off to wonder why I didn't think of it. I could have made that video. I *should* have made that video. Whilst pondering, I'll probably have a glass of wine to commiserate. Then again, maybe I'll just watch an unboxing video – I've heard the effect is the same.

"WHERE'S SIAN?" – THE IMPORTANCE OF FEMALE FRIENDSHIPS

KATIE STEED

When I was five, my best friend was Sian Divers. Sian beat me at pretty much everything: she was taller than me, she was reading books with blue stickers on when I was still stuttering through ones with green stickers, and she was considerably closer to being able to sit on her own hair – the sum of our joint ambitions – than I ever was.

But there was one thing I was always a tiny bit better than Sian at, and that was running. Kiss chase, tag, stuck in the mud – everyone else might have been playing with a smile on their faces and a song in their hearts, but I was studying. Gathering evidence. Discovering the one thing I could finally beat her at.

This was why, standing at the start line on our first ever sports day, my young heart was filled with what could be considered an arrogant over-confidence. Sian on the right of me, Heidi Stockley – barely a threat – on the left. I'd practised. I'd trained. I was ready.

We assumed the starting position. That hastily home-printed certificate had my name on it, I was sure of it.

The gun fired.

And Sian shot off like the entire cast of Jurassic Park *was behind her!*

Unknown muscles propelled her forwards; arms pumping, legs flying, body moving in perfect streamline motion across the finish line.

Sian came first, and I, having spent the first few seconds of the race with my chin on the floor, was beaten in to third place by Heidi *!*%* Stockley.

Looking back now, it's hard to see how our friendship survived this most traumatic of events, but survive it did: my friendship with Sian outlasted school, relationships, fads and fashions, because – to quote the inestimable My Little Pony, "Friendship is Magic" and we need to do a better job of representing it.

Psychologist Shelley Taylor said "beginning in early childhood, girls develop more intimate friendships than boys do and create larger social networks for themselves. Groups of women share more secrets,

disclose more details about their lives and express more empathy and affection for one another." We are failing to properly represent what is often the most important part of a young girl's life – the best friend.

That women are dramatically underrepresented in children's media is a long-established fact (they make up around 35% of onscreen characters). While there has been a heartening recent effort to make those female characters less passive, less stereotyped, and less defined by their relationships with men, the scarcity of female characters means that they rarely actually get to *talk* to each other, let alone form friendships, onscreen.

Female friendships, when they are depicted, bear little resemblance to Shelley Taylor's description, or to the mutual trust and camaraderie that make up screen versions of male friendships. They are filled with negative emotions, or, more specifically,

with one negative emotion: envy.

This issue, often referred to as the Smurfette Principle, comes up time and again across the media: women are presented as different and/or interesting purely because of their gender, and judged only in relation to their relationships with men. When another woman is introduced, the first is envious – her uniqueness is under threat, her very survival and what little power she has is derived from her relationships with men.

The media that children consume shapes who they become. Apart from the fact that it's pretty boring to see the same single emotion being rehashed again and again, it is my worry that this lack of representation is making itself known in boardrooms and offices around the world too.

Women have long been accused of not helping one another up the corporate ladder. The image of the "queen bee" who fights hard to reach the top but then sees all other women as competition is a pervasive stereotype, and one that makes sense when we are constantly shown that only one woman is allowed "in" at a time. This is the danger of tokenism.

In a world where women serve as CEOs of just 5% of the Fortune 500 companies, and make up just 15% of the boards, such are the consequences.

Negative emotions drive plots, and are an important part of how we teach young minds to express their feelings and empathize with others. No one wants to see episode after episode of hand holding and hair braiding, but the emotions used to drive female-centred plots are narrow stereotypes that pervade all media – women are jealous, backstabbing, bitter and totally willing to throw each other under a bus. I have felt every negative emotion under the sun towards Sian: anger, guilt, hurt, fear – any of these could drive a plot – but I've only once felt anything akin to envy, and that was when she beat me at running when I was five years old.

It makes an ok story, but it's not the *only* story.

VALUES ARE THE NEW BLACK!

DAVID HALLAM

I can hardly believe a year has passed since my business partner and good buddy Jon Hancock was sharing his thoughts on leaving the BBC and starting up our Indie co-venture – Three Arrows Media. One year on we are still plying our trade so I suppose that's something of an achievement!

In his article last year, Jon highlighted "The Value of Values" – he argued that it's the values underpinning our business that keep us on track, let others know what drives us and ultimately motivate us to achieve our goals.

One year on, little did I realize that *values* in their broader sense would suddenly become one of the buzzwords of the kids' TV business! I was lucky enough to hear the inspirational Kidscreen keynote speech from Harvard Professor Dr Richard Weissbourd, in which he championed the idea of kids' media promoting kindness and empathy. At around the same time there was the announcement of *Project Hope*, the co-venture between BBC Children's and Sky Kids which describes itself as a "kindness campaign". It was also this year that we announced our first major commission which just happens to be a show about values (more on that shortly).

As I contemplate our first year in business, I thought it might be enlightening (and perhaps a little scary!) to see the difference Three Arrows' values have made to our progress. Are our company values simply nice-sounding words that look good on a website or have they actually provided the framework to help us grow? There are six values which Jon and I feel are fundamental to Three Arrows:

- Collaboration
- Creativity
- Boldness
- Excellence
- Integrity
- Fun

Collaboration

The absolute necessity of collaboration is something that has dominated our first year. The majority of projects on our slate have been the result of collaborations – from like-minded producers as far afield as Australia to talent-driven concepts and industry specialists who bring particular expertise to a project. And it's not only the people who have generated content, it's the many, many lovely folk who have guided

our steps logistically, including our non-executive director, our legal advisor and our head of production. One of the best pieces of advice we were given when setting up the company was to surround ourselves with talented people and give them the space to do what they do best. Amen to that!

Boldness

This is one of those trickier values which I think most companies aspire to – hard to achieve because more often than not a producer's ability to be bold is governed by a broadcaster's willingness to be bold. In this regard, I feel that we have had our biggest "win" of the year. When Kay Benbow at CBeebies commissioned *Treasure Champs* in February, we embarked on this faith and values series for pre-schoolers that has boldness in its DNA – from a diverse cast, writing and production team, to the considerable challenge of making abstract concepts such as trust and respect accessible and fun for 4- to six-year-olds. And that's not to mention navigating the sensitivities of representing stories from six different faiths! We feel a huge sense of responsibility and gratitude for being given the opportunity to tackle this subject matter head on – watch this space for the results of our labours!

Creativity

There's no doubt that the last year has been a hugely creative time for the company. We have not only developed an exciting and diverse slate of projects but have also been fortunate enough to co-create one series which has been on air: *Asra*, a space-themed kids' gameshow for S4C. This is alongside the significant creative challenges of the CBeebies commission

– mixed media, kids, animals, religion … you do the maths!

One of the challenges of being creative within a small indie is staying focused on the "main thing". When you have the scope to conceive of anything you want, the danger lies in going off on tangents and not playing to your strengths. Creative freedom can be both a blessing and curse and this balancing act is something we are still learning to manage. The one thing we are absolutely convinced of is that we must keep high quality and ambitious creativity at the heart of everything we do.

Excellence

Whilst the excellence of our output is probably best judged by others, there's no doubt we are constantly striving for it. We are delighted to have welcomed into the Three Arrows family a wonderful production team of people from the rich talent pool of the North West. And it's not just *who* we've employed that is a mark of our pursuit of excellence, but all aspects of our day-to-day business: how people are treated, our internal systems, our external communications and timeliness in contracting and payments. This philosophy is probably best summed up in our company strapline – "Aim high".

Over the last year, Jon and I have been fortunate enough to sit on three award juries and it's a privilege to be in the position to celebrate and reward excellence in others, too.

Integrity

As Warren Buffet once said, "It takes 20 years to build a reputation and five minutes to ruin it – if you think about that you'll do things differently." Ask Tiger Woods, Lance Armstrong et al. As part of a partnership which has clocked up nearly 40 years in the business between us, this is a sobering thought and one that motivates us to place integrity at the heart of Three Arrows. What it boils down to is *treating others as you'd like to be treated* (I'm sure I've heard that somewhere before…) and staying true to who we are – even when it might be unprofitable or unpopular. Having this as one of our explicit values holds us to account both externally and to one another.

Fun

Finally, have we been able to have a laugh along the way and retain a sense of humour in the face of cashflow forecasts, tax returns and contract negotiations? Well, the honest answer is a definite "yes". The noise of a happy production team is a wondrous thing but there's no doubt that running a company is a bit of an emotional rollercoaster – one minute you're mini fist-pumping when a vaguely positive email comes through from a broadcaster and the next you're trying desperately to find a new way of writing "I don't suppose you've had a chance to look at our project, have you…?" It's not all gags and giggles but there's no doubt that retaining an ability to laugh is essential to surviving in the unpredictable world of kids' TV.

So, that's a whistle stop tour through the first full year of Three Arrows! Hopefully this goes some way to proving the point that values actually can play an important part in steering and growing a company.

Before I go, I'd like to salute the integrity of all the fabulously creative, collaborative, bold, excellent and fun people in children's media who make this such a brilliant sector to work in. Never forget the value of what you do!

EVERYTHING IS THE SAME, ONLY DIFFERENT: THE FUNDAMENTAL NEEDS OF CHILDREN

KATIE FRENCH

BBC younger audience needs model – a research study to understand the fundamental psychological needs of children to find out what their motivations and triggers are for accessing media and content.

As the famous saying goes, "The only thing that is constant is change", and for our children's audience we can all agree this is certainly true! The world children grow up in is constantly changing. The rise of a digital-first market has seen the emergence of a plethora of new online entertainment brands and content destinations. These have fostered the desire in children for more control and to access content on-demand, as well as leading to personalized and social experiences becoming increasingly appealing. As a content maker or commissioner, it can sometimes feel hard to keep up!

However, in the midst of these changes, it's important to remember that there is something that does stay the same: the fundamental needs of children. Children still have the same developmental stages and needs they have always had, it's just that the environment in which they satisfy these needs is evolving.

Why is this work on the needs of children important?

In an increasingly fragmented world, where content makers and brands are fighting for the attention of children, it is becoming more important for media, entertainment and content makers to take an audience-centric approach.

We need to ask the question – are we creating and commissioning content that truly meets the needs of children?

GENERAL CONTENT

Table 1: Core needs and sub-needs of children aged 2-15

Core Need	Sub Need
Ability: Need to explore individual skillset and learn more about the world.	**Learning & Discovery:** Help me learn and understand new things.
	Mastery: Help me improve my skills.
Independence: Need to become an independent being on the path to adulthood.	**Authority:** Help me gain control and influence over others.
	Self-expression: Help me to express myself.
	Identity: Help me to establish who I am & what I represent.
Social Connection: Need to interact with friends and family.	**Bonding:** Help me to get close to my family and learn how to behave with others.
	Acceptance: Help me fit in with my peers.
	FOMO: Help me to feel involved and part of the group.
Mood Management: Need to regulate mood and energy levels.	**Wind down:** Help me to relax.
	Stimulation: Help me to be actively engaged and entertained.
	Filling Time: Help me to fill time and be less bored.

What will this tell you?

It provides a simple framework of the psychological needs of younger audiences, explaining the motivations and triggers for accessing content and media and ultimately providing a springboard for content innovation.

What did we do?

There is a plethora of academic literature on this topic already, so the first stage aimed to utilize this knowledge through commissioning a literature review by Dr Adam Galpin[1]. Based on the literature, a framework of children's needs was developed.

The needs framework is fundamentally based on the academic literature, but we also conducted a second stage to develop the needs framework into something user friendly and easily accessible by content makers.

For the second stage we commissioned a children's specialist research agency, Crowd DNA, to conduct a longitudinal primary research study following a cohort of young people aged 2–24 over a six month period. The findings in this article are focused on the cohort of

In order to address this, it is important to understand the fundamental motivations and triggers that drive children's behaviour and media use. Although developmental stages are well documented, there is a clear lack of a straightforward audience-centric needs model. This work provides a framework to help content makers continue to create content and experiences that children need and love.

---
[1] Galpin, A. (2016). Towards a theoretical framework for understanding the development of media-related needs. *Journal of Children and Media, 10*(3), 385-391. http://www.tandfonline.com/doi/abs/10.1080/17482798.2016.1194373

those aged 2–15.

The aim was to explore both the conscious and unconscious needs of the children's audience, so observation research methodology was employed, as well as deprivation and exposure tasks and in-depth interviews with peers and families to understand how brands and content were meeting the needs.

What did we find?

The fundamental psychological motivations and triggers that drive children's behaviour and media use can be characterized into four core needs. Each core need has sub-needs which help to describe how the four needs play out across the age groups.

Table 1 sets out the core needs of children and how they break up into specific sub-needs.

Four Core Needs

The four needs are integral across all ages. However, the relative importance of the needs do shift as the audience gets older. For children under eleven years of age, the needs of **ability** and **independence** are central to their lives. Turning eleven heralds great change. At this point, the **social connection** need really becomes prevalent and **mood management** becomes a way to cope with the increasing demands and stress of school and exams.

Table 2: Sub-needs by age group

2–7 year-olds	8–11 year-olds	12–15 year-olds
Learning & Discovery	Mastery	Acceptance
Authority	Learning & Discovery	FOMO
Self-expression	Authority	Identity
Bonding	Self-expression	Authority
Wind Down	Identity	Killing/Filling Time
Stimulation	Acceptance	Wind Down
	Wind Down	Learning & Discovery
	Stimulation	Mastery
	Killing/ Filling Time	

Table 2 highlights which sub-needs are most important at the different ages.

2–7 year-olds

There are six key needs for the youngest children. Children aged 2–7 use various techniques such as imitation, role-play, questioning and exploration to fulfil needs of **learning & discovery** and **self-expression**. There is a huge desire to do things independently. Forms of technology (e.g. tablets) help children to exert control over their media choices and fulfil the **authority** need.

Parental needs

This research also explored the needs of parents and the most important parental need of all was **distraction**. Parents use media to help them get things done, whether that be housework, cooking tea, looking after other siblings or on the go in car journeys or day trips. Media that is portable and easy for children to use with minimal parental input really helps to meet this need. Other parental needs include: **learning and education, mood management** and **promoting good behaviour.**

8–11 year-olds

The challenge of engaging children becomes harder as they get older, as a result of increasing fragmentation of the market and the fact that children are gaining more control over their media consumption. Adding to the challenge is the growing amount of needs that these older children have – nine to be exact.

By the age of eight, although **learning & discovery** is still important, the **mastery** need starts to develop. At this point, children have a good foundation and breadth of knowledge and they now seek to gain depth of knowledge through mastering their skillset and pursuing more complex challenges.

As well as **mastery**, other new needs develop from eight onwards, including **identity** and **acceptance**, as children start to wrestle with concepts of who they are versus who they want to be and the desire to fit in with their peers.

12–15 year-olds

The age of eleven onwards heralds a period of great change and instability. Once they leave the familiar surroundings of primary school, children are faced by the daunting yet exciting prospect of secondary school. Their social world expands and the need for **social connection** and **acceptance** becomes very strong. It is also at this point that they usually get access to their own smartphone which fully opens up the world of social media. With it develops an insatiable desire to be "always on", characterizing what is well known as the **fear of missing out (FOMO)**. Children and teenagers do not want to miss out on what is going on with their friends and the world and are compelled to check their social media accounts any chance they get. This coincides with the ongoing development of their **identity** and use of social media to reflect on content they consume and the opinions of others to iteratively understand and develop who they want to be.

This generation has also grown up with the backdrop of austerity, rising costs of further education and no guarantee of a good job or ability to buy their own home in the future. As such, they are focused and seek to "get ahead" through hard work and ambition. In this context, the learning & discovery need shifts to focus on curriculum goals and passing exams. Increasing pressures to do well at school and the stress of exams means that media is used as a great way to **wind down.**

So, what's next?

The fundamental basis of this research is the long standing developmental literature, so it will be no surprise that as experts in children's media, a lot of content makers and commissioners of children's content will already be in tune with these psychological needs. However, the aim of this research is not to teach you to suck eggs but to provide a user friendly framework and invite content makers and commissioners to answer the question – **are we creating and commissioning content that truly meets the needs of children?**

We know from the research that, in some cases, content and brands are great at meeting certain needs. However, there are definitely gaps and opportunities, particularly as children get older.

- So, for the youngest children, how can you continue to offer ways in which they can interact and develop relationships with characters and brands to help express themselves and explore notions of identity?
- How can you ensure that products are easy to use for the youngest of children to help them gain authority, as well as meet the parental need to distract?
- As children get older, how can we better meet the mastery need and give children more opportunities to engage with their hobbies and interests?
- How can we ensure that children and teenagers have access to distinctive content that can help shape their identity, as well as give them ways to relax and escape increasing pressures of school and exams?

In a world where change is a certainty, let's ensure we evolve and adapt in a way that doesn't lose sight of those fundamental needs that will stand the test of time.

CHILDREN'S DOCUMENTARIES: *MY LIFE* – ALIVE AND WELL IN A DIGITAL WORLD

KEZ MARGRIE

The *My Life* single documentary strand is now in its ninth season on CBBC. The films follow the lives of some extraordinary children and the series has gained international recognition, winning awards across the globe. I'm lucky enough to be the BBC executive producer who looks after the strand. It's an immense privilege and I get to work with a fantastic range of passionate and dedicated indies who bring us the children and their stories. Some of the recent films we've commissioned have dealt with children coming to terms with the death of their mother (made by Big Deal), the hectic life of a junior vlogger facing major surgery (Blakeway North) and two brothers who live (literally) on a desert island (MCC Media).

As we all know, the way children engage with media is continually changing. When you consider some of the current broad-brush beliefs around how kids consume content, on the face of it *My Life* probably shouldn't exist. It isn't a format; every show is unique; there is no narrative arc or recurring character across a series; you can't turn it into merchandise or an app; and most of the films are 28 minutes long in an age where attention spans have supposedly evaporated.

These are big obstacles. And yet in 2016 the linear TV series did better than ever before, with each episode landing in the CBBC channel's top ten shows for that week. Even more gratifyingly, each episode was in the top 40 of the most-watched programmes on BBC iPlayer. That isn't the top 40 most-watched children's programmes on iPlayer, but the top 40 shows across the whole of the BBC's output.

How has this come about? Shouldn't documentary be dead in our hyper-competitive marketplace? Well, some things we know will resonate with any

generation – compelling stories, fascinating contributors, subject matter which is current and relevant. I believe that there are other reasons, too, some of them to do with how we've developed the strand on television over the past few years, and others centring around how we engage with the audience on digital platforms.

On TV

So, TV first: a key aim for us has been to give increasing power to the child contributors themselves. They do all the voice-overs and, while the video diary format is not new, as the first generation of digital natives, children in 2017 are very proficient at self-filming. The personal moments they capture are nearly always where the strongest and most emotional content comes from. Casting is also incredibly important. What all the *My Life* children have in common is a real self awareness and ability to tell their story in their own words. Grown-ups have to really earn their place in these films. They can be there to affirm what the contributor is saying, but certainly not to take over the narrative. This is a vital part of the commissioning criteria – these are not films *about* kids but *by* them.

How we handle tone has been an interesting journey too. The *My Life* films are constructed in classic documentary style, but that isn't the same as constructing them for documentary aficionados. We have to make the films engaging for young children who may not be familiar with the documentary format. I passionately believe that documentary is the strongest form of story-telling and if we are able to build the next generation of documentary lovers through the *My Life* brand, then job done! To that end, we use pop or commercial music tracks to help draw kids in to the stories, despite the sometimes gritty subject matter. We've been helped enormously in this by working with such a wide range of indies, often companies that are new to us, who bring great stories to the strand.

Other platforms

So, it does well on TV, but CBBC is more than a TV channel and in order to be relevant to and discoverable by children (and their parents), we have to ensure that there is a *My Life* presence on all our platforms, with BBC iPlayer key.

The strong stories that we feature really cut through on our celebrated on-demand service, and beyond the children's area too. The main documentaries category, and also the iPlayer homepage, will often feature episodes of *My Life* as they perform so well with the wider BBC audience. The *My Life* digital footprint on iPlayer is additionally enhanced through our ability to organize the films into a collection. It's a useful way of grouping all the unique episodes into a single place that our audience can discover and enjoy.

When it comes to the CBBC website, we work closely with the producers to choose short compelling moments from the films, giving a taster of what's to come each week to build excitement. We can now also do the same via CBBC's official YouTube channel, which gives us the benefit of being able to reach additional kids who may not be frequent viewers of CBBC or users of our website.

We also have activity on CBBC's Facebook page, which is where we are able to reach teens and parents. The nature of *My Life's* public service topics means that it does garner a wide interest, and presents opportunities for co-viewing. The older kids and parents we are able to reach on CBBC's Facebook page need something they can very quickly dip into. With the last series, we experimented with producing short one-minute films that get directly to the heart of the story. They come with embedded text, as we know that nearly 90% of people watching content on Facebook do so without any sound. We live in a world of "I want it now!" so if the one-minute short has excited someone to view the whole film, it needs to be available to them there and then. For that reason, we posted the shorts on Facebook only after the CBBC channel TX, so the episodes were ready and available on iPlayer. Pushing to a TX slot just wouldn't work in this space. So, did it work? Absolutely. The posts have regularly received tens of thousands of views.

We have experimented with Twitter in the same way, although only dipping our toe in the water. The built-in brevity of this platform presents us with a challenge, given the in-depth nature of our content. However, promoting specific moments of awe and fun seem to work, and it's something we may explore further for the next season.

On the subject of social media, it's worth mentioning how much more care we have had to take with our contributors in recent years. These are real kids, not actors, and given the nature of some of their stories, we have to be sure that they and their families are robust enough to cope with the potential interest in them on social media. All families are carefully briefed before participation, and know who to contact should anything arise that they need help with. We expect to have an ongoing dialogue with them about our safeguarding advice throughout the production process and beyond.

To date, despite the sometimes challenging nature of these films, the overwhelming response has been very positive. In general, people recognize that the contributors themselves have the right to tell their stories. However, the darker side of trolling and cyber bullying is always a risk, and we try to be as prepared as possible.

The advantages and disadvantages of the digital world, along with my interest in child-centric content, will also feature in a session that I'm producing for the Children's Global Media Summit on 5–7 December in Manchester. This event is the latest incarnation of the World Summit on Media for Children conferences, which have taken place around the globe every three years since 1995. It is coming to Manchester for the first time.

One of the five broad themes that we are exploring at the summit is empowerment, and how children's media can give kids a bigger voice on the global stage, along with what role it may play in fostering or combating our unconscious biases. *My Life's* diverse range of contributors is one of its key strengths, and a subject close to my heart. I'm looking forward to drawing this out in the session that we are planning.

Do please visit http://cgms17.com if you'd like to find out more. And look out for season 10 of *My Life* on CBBC in 2018!

NOSTALGIA

MUSICAL YOUTH: MY UNLIKELY HEROES OF THE 80S

CHRIS BANKS

—

It seems that every other week, Channel 5 shows a retrospective of the 1980s. Coiffured New Romantics queuing up for the Blitz Club, pin-striped yuppies yelling into bricks, Duran Duran camping it up on yachts. But that's not the 1980s I remember.

I was in primary school throughout the decade, surviving in a Welsh village so remote you couldn't even receive FM radio. No Top 40 home-taping for me. My musical upbringing came from just two sources: my parents' old record collection (mostly Beatles, Monkees and the complete works of Gilbert & Sullivan) and those golden hours between four and six every evening – children's television.

In those early years, my influences weren't The Jam, The Cure, or The Police, they were *Grange Hill*, *Terrahawks*, *The Mysterious Cities Of Gold*, *Bertha*, *Gruey*, *Jossy's Giants*, *Simon and the Witch*. I'd record the theme tunes onto cassettes and work them out on the piano. Find me a keyboard now and I'll serenade you with a medley of Jonathan Cohen's greatest hits: *Play Away*, *Rentaghost* – I even do a passable *Galloping Galaxies!*

By the end of the decade, I was taking my hard-earned pocket money to Woolworths, striding purposefully past the latest Kylie and Jason albums towards the "Other" section at the back of the shop. My bounty: *World Of TV Themes*, *Best Of BBC Children's TV*, *TV's Greatest Hits* – whatever compilations I could lay my ten-year-old mitts on. Saturday afternoons were spent cross-legged against the hi-fi speaker, in thrall to the music of *Captain Zep*, *Mop and Smiff* and *Think Again*, again and again.

To my pre-teen ears, these tunes were more powerful than any pop record. I couldn't articulate what it was that made the reggae groove of Benni Lees' *Pigeon Street* so irresistible, nor the strains of Kerr and Faulkner's *Bagpuss* so melancholic. But the answer was simple – the composers cared. Yes, they were writing "for children", but perhaps that's the very reason they cared so much. Their formula: musically encapsulate the feel and intent of the show you precede, imbue your melodies and lyrics with a virulent ear-worminess, make no harmonic concessions for your young audience, and task good musicians with playing great arrangements on real instruments. That's the way you create a formative soundtrack that for some, like me, would last a lifetime.

It's the standard to which we current kids' composers aspire. Paul Moessl's catchy music for *The Numtums* shares a sonic sensibility with *Sesame Street*. Listen to our punchy *ZingZillas* theme and you'll spot rhythmic echoes of *Jamie and the Magic Torch*. *Byker Grove* sounded fresh and contemporary back in the late 80s, just as *4 O'Clock Club* does now. Oasis called it "Standing On The Shoulders Of Giants". But where are those giants now, and why aren't they better remembered?

A few years ago, my composing partner Wag and I worked on the annual *CBeebies Christmas Show*. The honour was made all the greater when we were asked to write a song for our childhood hero, Derek Griffiths. Perhaps better known as a legendary TV presenter, Griffiths is also a multi-instrumentalist and composer. The hilarious post-rehearsal curry at which he regaled us with his memories of *Bod* and *Heads and Tails* is an evening we'll cherish forever. He was humbled when I gushed about the influence his music has had on ours and we made it our mission to get him recognition.

With the aid of fellow composer Paul Farrer, we successfully campaigned for Griffiths to be awarded a BASCA Gold Badge for his services to music, alongside other notable greats from the pop and rock industry: Bob Geldof, Kate Rusby, Alison Moyet. But at the Savoy ceremony, it was Griffiths who received the warmest reception, including impromptu tributes from Radio 2's Jo Whiley and Anne Dudley, ex-Art of Noise member. Kids' TV composers may not share the glamour of pop stars, but their music can last just as long.

Derek Griffiths is one of many. When I look back at the 1980s, I don't think of your Spandau Ballets, your Bananaramas, your Whams. I think of Derek Griffiths, Jonathan Cohen, Mike Amatt, Pete Gosling, Johnny Douglas, Benni Lees, Freddie Phillips, John Faulkner, Sandra Kerr, and all the other brilliantly creative songwriters who helped shape the musical tastes of children like me. They may not appear in Channel 5 retrospectives – most of them aren't even household names. But their music inspired the next generation of TV composers. They are the real heroes of my musical youth.

NOSTALGIA

AND THEY CALL IT PUPPET LOVE

WARRICK BROWNLOW-PIKE

At the age of two, I happened to see *The Muppet Show* on television and immediately my fate was sealed. I was completely captivated and my obvious fascination inspired my parents to buy me my first puppet. It was from that moment that my passion for performing began and was to become my career.

I would puppeteer for anyone who would watch. I dreamed of working with the Jim Henson Company, with the Muppets and on *Sesame Street*. I scoured magazines and television programmes and read and watched everything that I could, to learn exactly how the puppets worked. My mum Jacqui would take me all over the UK, to any venue that was holding puppetry exhibitions or screenings, because her puppet-obsessed son couldn't get enough!

By the age of about eight, I started to get frustrated with my shop-bought puppets, realizing how limiting their expressions and capabilities were. So, my mum and I began to work out how to build our own. With scraps of foam and fabric (and many glue gun burns) we learned how to bring to life the characters I'd held in my imagination for so long. This was a massive leap, from watching characters on television, to creating characters of my own.

After many years of mastering my craft at home, I decided the time was right to take the leap and audition for a TV show. That first audition was for *Space Pirates*, on CBeebies. I got the job and since that first lucky break, I've been working professionally non-stop.

Over the past ten years I have racked up hundreds of hours of air time, working with the BBC Children's Presentation team on series like *Ed and Oucho's Excellent Inventions*, *Transmission Impossible*, *Hacker Time*, *Spot Bots*, *Get Well Soon* and BBC Three's *Mongrels*. It all came full circle in 2013 when I began working with the very same company that had originally inspired me at the age of two! I got a job working on The Jim Henson Company and BBC's *That Puppet Game Show*. Dream fulfilled.

Other highlights have seen me become Elmo from *Sesame Street*'s right-hand man in the UK, and a lead performer in the Sesame Workshop/CBeebies co-production *The Furchester Hotel*. It was on this show that I was given the opportunity to develop my very own character, Gonger, the little furry pink chef.

In 2014, I was selected as one of only four full-time core UK Muppet performers for the most recent Muppets film, *Muppets Most Wanted*, with Ricky Gervais, Ty Burrell and Tina Fey. It was here I got to perform my childhood favourites such as Fozzie Bear, whenever Fozzie's regular performer was busy working Miss Piggy.

For the past seven years, I have had the pleasure of being able to perform and develop my character, Dodge T Dog, and I love every minute of it. He presently resides in the CBeebies House and gets to entertain, with my help, thousands of adoring preschoolers on the CBeebies channel every day.

This year I flew to New York City, where I became a member of the *Sesame Street* Muppet performers team for *Sesame Street*'s forty-eighth season. Working on a show which has inspired me for such a long time is humbling – I feel so privileged that, every day, I'm doing what I've wanted to do since I was two years old.

I recently set up my own puppet-based production company called Planet Pumpkin, so I can take the next step in my career by developing and producing my own ideas. I'll always want to be a puppeteer and I'll always want to create engaging content that entertains people. It's the best job in the world.

NOSTALGIA

A TWINKLY TIME, LONG, LONG AGO...

SIMON PARTINGTON

One of the best bits of working in animation is getting the opportunity to design the world and characters for a brand-new series. A blank canvas is so exciting and it's an even sweeter prospect when the project allows you to draw on the TV shows that you adored as a child. With the production of the CBeebies programme *Old Jack's Boat* and the subsequent spin-off *Old Jack's Boat: Rock Pool Tales*, nostalgia has never been far away. It has been lovely to think back regularly to my own childhood viewing and ponder what is was about those classics that meant so much to me then, and still inspires me today.

One of the first connections I can remember having with animation was with *Dougal and the Blue Cat*. My love for *The Magic Roundabout*, and this beautiful film in particular, started back in the late 1970s when my mum and dad would play an LP of the narrated soundtrack from the film to me and my sister.

I had one point of reference for the look of the film at the time – a single image of the characters lined up on the record sleeve. The wonderful Buxton the cat standing amongst Florence, Dougal, Dylan and the other more familiar residents of the magic garden really caught my imagination. I can still clearly remember lazy afternoons sat around the record player listening to the story play out, imagining images to accompany Eric Thompson's marvellous narration.

Fast forward to 2010 and the fully restored film was released on DVD. I finally sat down to see the film I'd been imagining for the past 30 years or so. The film was brilliant, of course – that didn't surprise me – but I wasn't prepared for it to be such a nostalgic experience. It brought back memories of cream and brown patterned carpets and curtains, white plastic record players with slightly fuzzy speakers and happy feelings of me sitting in the family home with my parents and sister.

As I watched, it was interesting to compare the images I imagined as a child against the director's vision, and to see how I had misunderstood or wrongly imagined certain scenes. It surprised me how much of the dialogue I could still recite from the film even though it was years since I had heard it.

What part this early introduction to an animated property had on my choice of career is unclear, but what I am sure of is that this created world and others like it (*The Wombles*, *Chorlton and the Wheelies*, *The Flumps*, *Bagpuss* and *Ivor the Engine*) seemed to fuel my fertile childhood imagination and have continued to inspire my own artistic attempts throughout the years.

It was such a privilege to be involved in the early discussions for *Old Jack's Boat* with the in-house production team at CBeebies and to play a part in developing a brand-new world for its core audience whilst, hopefully, bringing warm and nostalgic feelings to the fore for parents and grandparents alike.

The chance to work with Bernard Cribbins (performing Old Jack himself!) was a dream come true for a huge fan of *The Wombles*. The man who created the memorable voices for the much beloved stop motion series would now be performing new voices for the characters my team and I were designing and animating. This was a very exciting prospect for all involved!

It's still a thrill to get the rushes (raw footage) back from the edit and listen to how Bernard has perceived the animated cast from the early illustrations we provided. So much of the animated performance, movement and personality is dictated by the life he breathes into the characters. His performance and perfect delivery of the stories have the ability to transport people back to perhaps a simpler time, and I feel that this is a big part of the show's heart and appeal.

I recall discussion in the early development of the show about having an animation style that gave a nod to children's television of the past. So, we worked on a "cut-out" style, deciding on charm over glossiness. The animation style is limited in many ways (there is no perspective, for example) but it feels totally at home with the simplicity and setting of the programme.

A deliberately handmade feel to the art direction was developed using a mixture of photographs, textures and craft materials to give a very illustrative aesthetic to the world, all in an attempt to design something that hopefully harks back to the way animations used to be made.

I know the whole team at Flix Facilities are very thankful to be involved in such a beautiful CBeebies production and it is wonderful to see all the work, love, care and attention that goes into every process of making each *Old Jack's Boat* story. A combined 85 episodes, 2 specials

and 2 BAFTAs later, the show certainly seems to continue to find its audience. I have heard of families sitting down together to watch and enjoy it which is such a lovely thought – and I even know of a few big kids who watch it whether the children are in or not!

My hope is that in 30 years' time, children watching now may remember *Old Jack's Boat* with the same fondness and affection that I feel for the television of my own childhood – those warm and fuzzy feelings of nostalgia that can transport us back to another place and time – or, as Old Jack would say, to "A twinkly time, long, long ago".

FAREWELL

JOHN NOAKES: A TRIBUTE

RICHARD MARSON

In 2005, a special dinner was held for all five Blue Peter editors up to that point, myself included, together with Edward Barnes, another of the programme's founding fathers, and a one-time deputy and head of the children's department. During the evening, talk turned inevitably to which had been the most successful and effective presenters. The unanimous feeling around the table was that, despite some tough and talented competition, the greatest presenter of them all had been John Noakes.

However, it could all have been a different story, and indeed, Noakes' television career very nearly came to an ignominious end just a few months after he landed his first *Blue Peter* contract, towards the end of 1965. Like many other presenters before and since, he'd worked as an actor, and he found it a special form of agony transitioning to a job in which he principally had to be himself. "This glass eye, the camera, stripped me naked," he later commented. "I actually shook with fear, the voice tremoring as I said the words. The first few months were quite terrifying. I went through murder. I even went to a hypnotist and a faith healer to try to get me out of it."

"I don't think he looked at the right camera once," remarks Edward Barnes, who was then the senior producer on *Blue Peter*. "It was painful to watch. I remember one time we had a very smart, very upright Corporal of Horse from the army in the studio. Noakie got completely lost during the item and asked him, "Have you got any idea what's coming next?"

"No, Sir!" shouted the Corporal of Horse.

"Nor have I," shrugged Noakes. "And it's getting to be quite a problem!"

Noakes was actually dropped from the 1966 summer expedition, and serious consideration was given to dropping him from the programme itself. But then, at last, everything began to click. He started to develop "this idiot, who is not really the real John Noakes. I'd got rid of my Yorkshire accent at drama school. I brought it back and used it as part of a character."

Now, instead of cringing at the procession of mishaps and mistakes, the audience was let in on the joke, and began to relax and enjoy Noakes' natural anarchy and boyish charm. If, as he later claimed, his marathon stint of 12 and a half years on *Blue Peter* was mostly just a performance, then it was one of the greatest sustained examples of television acting ever. His bravery, his subversive sense of humour and his celebrated relationship with four-legged companions, first Patch and then, from 1971, Shep, proved an irresistible combination. If Valerie Singleton was rather like a member of the royal family, then Noakes was the comedy footman, frequently stumbling and making mistakes, and bringing a genuine warmth and humour to the twice-weekly programmes. When a baby elephant called Lulu famously visited the studio in the summer of 1969, Noakes added to the chaos, exclaiming "Get off me foot!" He later admitted that the poor animal hadn't actually trodden on him at all, he had simply seized the opportunity to borrow the catchphrase of the now-forgotten comedian Frank Randle, who had been popular when Noakes was a lad.

But, as well as acting the clown, Noakes also defined the role of the action presenter. He seemed utterly fearless, claiming that his feats of supreme bravery were possible only because he had "no imagination" and that he was only ever truly scared on two occasions: once while trying out a vertiginous tree swing, the other while trying to remain atop a circus sway pole. Health and safety were then in their infancy so these films were approached with a mixture of common sense, working with

FAREWELL

the experts and a hefty dose of pure luck. Indeed, one steeplejack film which Noakes made in his final months on the programme was never shown because, tragically, the man in charge fell to his death shortly after the filming.

One of his early edge-of-the seat achievements was his ascent to the towering mast of HMS Ganges. It was extremely hazardous and indeed, just a few years later, the entire exercise was abandoned due to the mortality rate among the naval cadets who had to master it as part of their training. Noakes nearly made it to the top but, totally exhausted, was forced to give in at the very last minute, giving him the unwelcome headache of changing places with a cadet 38.7 metres from the ground. Biddy Baxter, the show's editor at the time, felt it "... was almost better than him getting there because it gave encouragement to all the viewers who never quite won the race

or came top in the exam. Their hero, John, admitting defeat."

His other remarkable adventures are too many to list but the highlights include dodging out of the way of the erupting Mount Etna, completing a four-mile high freefall with the RAF Falcons, scaling one of the towers of Fulham Power station, coming off a bobsleigh at high speed (he showed off the impressive bruises to his backside back in the studio) and, perhaps the most celebrated of them all, climbing to the very top of Nelson's column. He actually did this twice – first in 1968 and then again in 1977, a jaw-dropping piece of film which has been repeated countless times since, and which never loses its power to shock and impress. The director was Alex Leger, who recalls: "John made it all the way to the top via a series of ladders roped to the sides, with no harness of any kind. But the really tricky part was when he reached the overhang of the plinth at the top. Climbing the ladders here meant supporting his full weight too. Then, when he'd finally made it, the sound recordist told me that there had been a technical problem so he would have to go back and do it again. Noakes didn't moan; he just got on with it. He was incredibly brave."

This was the era of three channels only, so his antics were enjoyed by a vast captive audience which sometimes reached the dizzy heights of eight or nine million people

– unthinkable now. In 1975, there was a spin-off series, *Go with Noakes*, built around the mammoth popularity he enjoyed, in which he (and Shep) explored the highways, byways and coastlines of the UK, trying out all kinds of activities along the way. Noakes eventually left *Blue Peter* in the summer of 1978, having appeared in more than 1,000 programmes. He returned to make special appearances for the 35th, 40th and 50th anniversaries of the programme, as well as to help dig up a time capsule in 2000, when he and his fellow presenter Peter Purves were both honoured with the programme's highest award, a gold badge.

However, it is no secret that Noakes' departure from *Blue Peter* was tinged with bitterness and rancour, principally over the ownership of Shep. Like most of the programme's pets, Shep officially belonged to the BBC. When Noakes left, he was offered the chance to keep the dog on one condition – that he didn't use him in any advertising. Noakes refused the condition and Shep was retired to live with the programme's then animal handler, Edith Menezes. It broke Noakes' heart and, in years to come, he became tearful on more than one occasion when discussing Shep and their separation. When he looked back over his departure from the show which had forever cemented his name with the British public, Noakes admitted that he was "exhausted. The pressure was terrible. I'd done all these things and I don't think any of them really realized how difficult it was. It was a Peter Pan existence, a bit like an overgrown schoolboy's job."

By the end of his extraordinarily long stint, he may have been exhausted, but he was also undoubtedly *Blue Peter*'s superstar, his achievements unsurpassed by anyone who followed him. News of his death, after a long battle with dementia, unleashed a huge outpouring of deep affection and respect. For many, John Noakes was a definitive and inspiring part of their childhood – a funny, tenacious, down-to-earth hero whose bravery and jokes made life better and anything seem possible.

PETER SALLIS: A TRIBUTE

NICK PARK

I'm so sad, but feel so grateful and privileged to have known and worked with Peter over so many years. He was always my first and only choice for Wallace. I knew him of course from the very popular long running BBC series Last of the Summer Wine. He brought his unique gift and humour to all that he did, and encapsulated the very British art of the droll and understated.

Working with Peter was always a delight and I will miss his wry, unpredictable humour and silliness – that started the moment he greeted you at the door, and didn't stop when the mic was switched off. He had naturally funny bones and was a great storyteller and raconteur off stage too and would keep us amused for hours. He could make the simplest incident sound hilarious – just by the way he said it.

When I look back I'm so blessed and fortunate that he had the generosity of spirit to help out a poor film school student back in the early 1980's, when we first recorded together, when neither of us had any idea what Wallace & Gromit might become.

Peter's unique, charming quality, together with oversized vowels and endearing performance, helped me fashion Wallace from the beginning; the way he first said "We've forgotten the Crackers Gromit" and "Cracking toast Gromit" or just "Cheeeese!" soon lead to Wallace's enormous "coat-hanger mouth".

They don't come along very often like Peter Sallis – he was a unique character, on and off screen, and an absolute honour to have known him

MYKE CROSBY
1961 – MAY 2017

KARL WOOLLEY

The industry lost one of its finest when Myke Crosby sadly passed away on 18 May this year.

Myke was an inspirational and passionate producer of kids' TV and digital content having worked at Fox Kids, Prism Entertainment and Bin Weevils where he created and built the hugely successful kids online world of the same name. Everything Myke touched bore the hallmarks of his wonderful personality: fun, irreverence, wide-eyed engagement, an infectious smile and a wry laugh at the world. Myke never talked down to the kids he entertained because at heart he'd never really grown up himself. He will be sadly missed by his wife, Amelia, his beautiful daughter, Natasha, and all of us who'd had the great privilege to meet him and work with him.

CONTRIBUTORS

Margret Albers

Margret has been CEO of the German Children's Media Foundation GOLDENER SPATZ and director of the Media Festival of the same name from 1996 to 2016. She is the board spokeswoman of the Association for the Promotion of German Children's Film. Together with Thomas Hailer and Greg Childs, she is responsible for the direction of studies at the Academy for Children's Media. She is also project director for the initiatives Outstanding Films for Children and Television from Thuringia. In addition, she is president of the European Children's Film Association (ECFA).

Laverne Antrobus

Laverne is a consultant child and educational psychologist and has worked with children and families in most need of help over the last 20 years. Having trained at the prestigious Tavistock Clinic in London, she then worked in local authorities and now for the NHS. Laverne appears on popular daytime broadcasts and is often asked to give a psychological perspective on issues that affect children and their families in both radio and print media. She has made programmes on childhood for the BBC and currently appears on the CBeebies Grown-ups website. This year she will be joining the team of psychologists on the Channel 4 programme *Secret Lives of Five Year Olds*.

Cary Bazalgette

Cary worked at the British Film Institute from 1979 to 2007, having been a teacher of English and filmmaking in London secondary schools. She wrote and edited a number of classroom resources for media education and published and spoke widely on this topic in the UK and around the world. As head of BFI Education from 1999–2006, she led the development of new approaches to teaching and learning about moving-image media for the 3–14 age group. She is now undertaking doctoral research at the Institute of Education, London, on pre-school children's encounters with moving-image media. www.carybazalgette.net

Rebecca Atkinson

Rebecca is a children's writer and creative consultant specializing in the representation of disability in children's industries. She is the founder of toylikeme.org and listed in the 2017 Power100 list of influential disabled people for her work in this field. #ToyLikeMe is an arts and play based not-for-profit celebrating disability representation in toys and calling on the global toy industry to better represent 150 million children worldwide with disability and difference. toylikeme.org.

Chris Banks

Chris is one half of Banks & Wag, the award-winning London based TV composers with credits including *Go Jetters*, *Blue Peter*, *Friday Download*, *Wanda and The Alien*, and *ZingZillas*. www.banksandwag.com

Warrick Brownlow-Pike

Warrick's passion for performing began when he was two, whilst watching Jim Henson's *Muppets*. His credits include *Ed and Oucho*, *Hacker Time*, *Get Well Soon*, BBC Three's *Mongrels* and Henson's *That Puppet Game Show*. Warrick is a lead performer on *The Furchester Hotel* and was a core UK Muppet performer for the movie *Muppets Most Wanted*. Currently he is Dodge the Dog in the CBeebies House and has just returned from working on *Sesame Street* in New York. As well as a puppeteer, Warrick is an accomplished illustrator and puppet designer and is constantly developing new ideas for his production company Planet Pumpkin.

Helen Brunsdon

Helen is director of Animation UK. She has extensive experience in the animation industry as a BAFTA-winning producer of short films, television series, festivals and events. She has worked with some of the most creative talent in the UK including Aardman, Joanna Quinn, Arthur Cox, Brothers McLeod and as an executive producer she has worked with CBBC, Disney UK and CITV. Helen has a passion for nurturing talent and since 2014 has been an associate for Creative Skillset working across the animation, VFX and games sectors. She is also a visiting tutor and advisor for several universities, a member of festival advisory boards, events producer, co-host of *Show Me the Animation* and director of Animation Associates.

Greg Childs

Greg spent over 25 years at the BBC as a researcher, director, producer and executive producer – mainly in the children's department. Following a TV career producing *Play School* and *Record Breakers* (amongst others), he developed the first BBC websites and interactive television for children, and as head of children's digital he created the children's channels CBBC and CBeebies. After leaving the BBC, Greg consulted on digital innovation and management strategies for production companies and broadcasters across the world. His clients included Disney, the DfES, Al Jazeera Children's, CITV, Teachers TV, ITN, Avid and the European Broadcasting Union. Greg is the co-creator and editorial director of the Children's Media Conference, now in its fourteenth year in Sheffield. He is also one of the heads of studies at the German Akademie Für Kindermedien, and is the founding director of the Children's Media Foundation.

Tim Clague

Tim is a BAFTA-nominated writer and winner of the Jerwood Film Prize and works in games, TV and film. His work as writer/director has been broadcast on BBC 1, Channel 5 and ITV. Recently he has moved into children's content and has been directing commercials and early years' development material as well as promotional material for LEGO and Star Wars. He recently wrote for the CITV show *Oddbods* and RTE's *I'm a Fish* and is currently lead writer on a new computer game. He co-wrote and co-directed the live action children's feature film *Who Killed Nelson Nutmeg?* alongside Danny Stack. They have since set up Nelson Nutmeg Pictures Ltd with Jan Caston and are the UK's only production company that exclusively produces live action children's films.

Dr Barbie Clarke

Barbie is the founder of award-winning research agency Family Kids & Youth and was formerly a director at GfKNOP. Barbie completed her PhD in child and adolescent psychosocial development at the University of Cambridge, Faculty of Education, where her published research has looked at early adolescents' use of digital media. She taught postgraduate students at the faculty for five years. She is a trained child therapist and has worked with young offenders and in secondary schools in Tower Hamlets. A fellow of the Market Research Society (MRS), Barbie regularly writes articles and gives papers at international conferences, and has appeared on TV and radio commenting on youth research.

Alison David

Alison is consumer insight director at Egmont, the UK's leading specialist children's publisher of books and magazines and home to many of the world's favourite stories, best-loved authors and illustrators and characters including Thomas & Friends, Disney Princess, Disney Frozen, Star Wars™, LEGO®, Teletubbies, Michael Morpurgo, Enid Blyton, Julia Donaldson, Lemony Snicket, Michael Grant, Andy Stanton, Winnie-the-Pooh, Tintin, Mr Men, Stampy Cat and Minecraft. Alison has worked in the media and publishing industry for over 30 years and with research as a creator, analyst and end user. Through her extensive research, and as a parent herself, Alison has a real insight into the challenges facing reading. Her research programme at Egmont includes "Reading Street", a longitudinal study investigating children's reading and the environment in which they grow up to understand what it takes to inspire them to read for pleasure; a consumer segmentation study sizing the

CONTRIBUTORS

children's book and magazine market and identifying the motivations and aspirations of parents in regard to their children's reading for pleasure, "Print Matters", an exploration into parents' and children's responses to reading children's books, including print books, eBooks, apps and magazines and most recently "Print Matters More", a groundbreaking study that turned reluctant readers into enthusiasts in just 6 weeks. Alison is also the author of *Help Your Child Love Reading*, a practical guidebook for parents to help them inspire their children to read for pleasure.

Yara Farran

Yara is currently pursuing a Master's in Media and Communications at the London School of Economics, after completing a Bachelor in Arts and Science at McMaster University. Her interests are primarily in media identity and youth literacy, representation, and participatory modes of development. Alongside her current posts as a co-editor of the Children's Media Foundation newsletter and an editorial board member of UnMediated, the LSE's journal of politics and communications, she has assisted in pedagogical projects to increase accessibility and community engagement in higher education; community development projects within the arts and culture sector; and grassroots youth-led initiatives.

Katie French

Katie is currently head of the children's and learning audience team at the BBC. She ensures that research and audience insight informs the design and continuous development of products and services for flagship brands like CBeebies, CBBC and BBC Bitesize, to ensure these brands remain fit for purpose in a digital age. Prior to working in media research, Katie worked in the healthcare sector and headed up a market research team at the National Institute for Health and Care Excellence (NICE). She started her career as a health researcher for organizations such as the National Institute for Health Research and is published in the area of self-care and mental health.

David Hallam

David co-founded Three Arrows Media. Before this, he headed up development for three blue chip Indies: The Foundation/Zodiak Kids, Initial Kids/Endemol and Zenith Entertainment. He cut his teeth in production on seminal series such as *The Big Breakfast*, *The Word* and *GamesMaster*. For the last 20 years, he has been a development specialist across all kids' genres and demographics. David has been involved in the creation and development of over 30 series including *Fort Boyard: Ultimate Challenge*, *Scrambled!*, *Zack & Quack* and *Mister Maker's Arty Party*. Many of these series have gone on to be nominated or win national and international awards. David has an honours degree in Communication Studies with Education from the University of Middlesex and lives in Barnet, North London with his wife Clare and two children.

Anna Home OBE

Anna is chair of the CMF Board and a founding patron of the organization. She joined BBC radio in 1960 and started in children's television in 1964 where she worked as a researcher, then director, producer and executive producer, latterly specializing in children's drama. She started *Grange Hill*, the controversial school series. From 1981 – 86 she worked at the ITV company TVS where she was deputy director of programmes. In 1986, she returned to the BBC as head of children's programmes, responsible for all children's output. She revived the Sunday teatime classic dramas and one of her last decisions before retiring was to commission *Teletubbies*. After retiring from the BBC, Anna was chief executive of The Children's Film & Television Foundation until it merged into CMF in 2012. She has won many awards including a BAFTA lifetime achievement award. She was the first chair of the BAFTA Children's Committee, has chaired both the EBU Children's and Youth Working Group and the Prix Jeunesse International Advisory Board. Anna was the chair of the Save Kids' TV Campaign and the Showcomotion Children's Media Conference Advisory Committee. She now chairs the Board of the Children's Media Conference, and is a Board member of Screen South.

Dr Natalia Kucirkova

Natalia is a senior research fellow at the University College London Institute of Education. Her research concerns innovative ways of supporting children's book reading, digital literacy and exploring the role of personalization in early years. She developed an award-winning children's app, "Our Story", and is widely published on early literacy and children's technology. Her publications have appeared in *Communication Disorders Quarterly*, *First Language*, *Computers & Education* and *Cambridge Journal of Education*. She has been commended for her engagement with teachers and parents at a national and international level. Natalia currently leads an Economic and Social Research Council-funded project focused on children's personalized books.

Terri Langan

Terri started in children's media in 2011, following 15 years as a sport and factual producer and as head of development for indies in London and Manchester. After having twin boys and becoming increasingly absorbed in the programmes they watched, Terri joined BBC Children's in 2011 and led the CBeebies in-house development team for almost four years. Her commissions included BAFTA-winning series *Old Jack's Boat* as well as *Swashbuckle* and the RTS-award-winning *Stargazing*. Terri now runs Little Critics, a company developing and producing content specifically for a children's and family audience. She designs and leads children's media courses for Creative Skillset and is also a director of award-winning EYFS online numeracy scheme "Ten Town".

Sam Lawyer

Sam is a Master's student in Media and Communications at the London School of Economics and previously received her BA in English Literature from the University of Pennsylvania. Her current research focuses on comparative cultural studies of young digital media audiences in the US and UK. She is also co-editor of the monthly Children's Media Foundation newsletter and an editorial board member of UnMediated, the LSE's journal of politics and communications.

Estelle Lloyd

Estelle was born in France and spent most her career in New York and London. After early work in investment banking, she founded VB/Research in 2006. In 2014, she founded Azoomee, the app where kids can access hundreds of hours of content – TV, games, tutorial videos, audiobooks – in one secure place. It offers tailored, age-appropriate content that changes and develops as the child grows. The NSPCC is the company's founding partner and advisor on safety and parental controls.

Anne Longfield OBE

Anne was appointed children's commissioner for England in March 2015. In this role, she has legal responsibility for representing the views and interests of the nation's 12 million children to the decision-makers who can make a difference to their lives. She must also promote and protect their rights. Her work must focus on vulnerable groups of children in particular. Anne is a leading figure in the children's sector with over 30 years' experience of and expertise in shaping the national policy agenda and delivering services to children and families. She is passionate about championing children's interests and improving their lives and has led numerous high profile national campaigns, inquiries, commissions and research programmes that have effected positive change for children. Prior to becoming children's commissioner, Anne was chief executive of 4Children during which time she advised the government on children and family policy in the Prime Minister's Strategy Unit at Cabinet Office.

Nellie McQuinn

Nellie has been in the entertainment industry for over 20 years and has worked in Australia, New Zealand, UK and the USA. She joined Grass Roots Media as company director in 2006.

CONTRIBUTORS

Under Nellie's direction, the company has expanded into the digital media industry and now specializes in creating short form digital content for children. The company creates content for some of the most prolific children's brands and channels and the channels Nellie produces for have over seven billion views – a busy month can see her team producing over 300 videos!

Kez Margrie

Kez is a commissioning executive with independent production companies at CBBC. She is responsible for delivering factual and fact/ent content across all CBBC platforms. Kez looks after some of the channel's most successful factual brands including the multi-award-winning *My Life* series, the BAFTA-winning *Operation Ouch!*, *Our School* and *Ice Stars*. She has a background in production and now works closely with independent companies to produce the best, most relevant content across all our platforms for 6- to 12-year-olds in the UK.

Richard Marson

Richard joined *Blue Peter* in 1997 and stayed for a decade, with four years as the programme's editor, during which he won a BAFTA. In 2007, he was executive producer of BBC Four's *Children's TV On Trial*. In 2012, he masterminded *Tales of Television Centre* for BBC Four. Since 2013, he has been an executive producer at Twofour, where his credits include four series of CBBC's *Our School*. His books include *Inside Updown: The Story of Upstairs, Downstairs*, *Blue Peter 50th Anniversary*, *Totally Tasteless: The Life of John Nathan-Turner* and *Drama and Delight: The Life of Verity Lambert*.

Lucy Murphy

Lucy was appointed the first head of kids' content at Sky in 2015. She is responsible for all of Sky's on demand kids' content, a library with a selection of over 5,000 episodes, including the Sky Kids app which successfully launched in March 2016. Since joining Sky, Lucy has started commissioning exclusive Sky original kids' content including brand-new episodes of family favourite *Morph*. Lucy has over 25 years' experience in producing and brand managing shows for children's and family audiences. As a producer, script editor and development executive, she has worked on over 500 episodes of children's shows ranging from hit CBeebies show *Bing Bunny*, family favourite *The Gruffalo* and Aardman's *Tate Movie Project*; working for a diverse slate of clients from small indies to major international media groups. Prior to joining Sky, Lucy held a role at Azoomee, a kids SVOD platform, as creative director and head of content.

Alison Norrington

Alison is founder and creative director of storycentral Ltd, specializing in thematic and experiential storytelling with global partners in entertainment. She is also a bestselling novelist, playwright and journalist and a PhD researcher with a Master's in Creative Writing and New Media. Alison is conference chair for StoryWorld Conference LA, executive producer of virtual reality sessions for CMC and a two-time TEDx speaker. She is a BAFTA Guru and member of the International Academy of Television Arts & Sciences, The Writers Guild of Great Britain and Women in Film & TV.

Kate O'Connor

Kate was the executive director and deputy CEO of Creative Skillset since its inception and was responsible for developing key industry partnerships, policy and strategy for the industries sector skills council. In January 2015, Kate established and now runs a successful consultancy practice specializing in education, training and skills in the creative industries and works with a range of clients in the UK and internationally. In November 2016, she was appointed executive chair of the newly formed Animation Council, now officially part of the UK Screen Alliance and representing key screen sectors including animation, VFX, studios, post-production and facilities. Kate is chair of the BFI Research Committee and a member of the BAFTA Learning and New Talent Committee.

Nick Park

Nick is a four-time Academy Award® winner, three in the category of Best Animated Short Film – *Creature Comforts*, *The Wrong Trousers* and *A Close Shave* and more recently in the category for Best Animated Feature Film for *The Curse of the Were-Rabbit*. All four films were created and produced at Aardman, where Park is a co-director with founders Peter Lord and David Sproxton. In 1996, Nick and Aardman were honoured with a BAFTA Special Award for Original Contribution to Television. In 1997, Park was awarded a CBE. He is currently directing his latest feature film *Early Man* with film partner STUDIOCANAL, set for global theatrical release in 2018. In 2016, Aardman celebrated its 40th anniversary.

Dr Becky Parry

Becky is assistant professor at the University of Nottingham in the School of Education, and is a member of the Centre for Research in Arts, Literacy and Creativity. Becky has extensive experience as a lead researcher in two key projects, "Tracking Arts Learning and Engagement" at the University of Nottingham and "Developing Media Literacy" at the University College of London Institute of Education. Becky's own research interests lie in children's storytelling across media forms and playful approaches to the teaching and learning of literacy. Her research focuses particularly on children's film and media as well as film and media education. She is author of *Children, Film and Literacy*, published by Palgrave Macmillan. Becky was formerly a teacher and cinema educator and has managed numerous international creative media production projects with children and young people. She has a strong interest in participatory and arts-based approaches to research with children and is keen to undertake research which creates impact, developing a socially just and more tolerant society.

Simon Partington

Simon is the head of animation at Flix Facilities Ltd. Simon has contributed to numerous animation and puppetry series including *Postman Pat: SDS*, *The Furchester Hotel* and *Toby's Travelling Circus*. He is the animation director and designer of the BAFTA-award- winning BBC children's series *Old Jack's Boat* and was producer and director of *Poppies*, a Remembrance Day film for CBeebies and CBBC.

Emma Scott

Emma is the founder and CEO of Beano Studios, a global kid's entertainment business based on the spirit and rebellion of the *Beano*. Emma was previously the managing director of Freesat, the UK's fastest-growing TV and on-demand service, and an ITV and BBC joint venture. Prior to founding Freesat, Emma was chief of staff to the BBC director-general, Greg Dyke, where she led the launch of Freeview, created the BBC's first on-demand digital platform, and established a new TV region. Emma began her career working as a researcher in the House of Commons for a Shadow Cabinet minister.

Kiley Sobel

Kiley is a PhD candidate and National Science Foundation graduate research fellow in Human Centered Design & Engineering at the University of Washington. She is interested in inclusion, design research, and assistive technology. Kiley's primary research is in understanding how interactive technology might help increase opportunities for children with diverse abilities and needs to equally, actively, and meaningfully participate in the same setting. She has also done assistive technology research with Microsoft Research, has volunteered as a teacher's assistant in early childhood education classrooms, and co-designs technology with children on an intergenerational design team called KidsTeam UW.

Katie Steed

Katie is an award-winning director and

CONTRIBUTORS

co-founder of animation production company Slurpy Studios, who produce animated content for commercial, educational and entertainment clients, ranging from BBC Learning to the British Council. Away from the studio, Katie is a well-travelled advocate of animation, guest teaching and mentoring at the NFTS, UCA Farnham and Falmouth, and has recently returned from a British Council-led initiative to educate and promote the Zimbabwean animation industry. Katie has a keen interest in furthering and bettering the representation of women and minorities in the media, and frequently writes for *Skwigly* animation magazine.

Professor Jeanette Steemers

Jeanette is Professor of Culture, Media and Creative Industries at King's College London. A graduate in German and Russian at the University of Bath, she completed her PhD on public service broadcasting in West Germany in 1990. After working for research company CIT Research and international television distributor HIT Entertainment, she rejoined academia in 1993. Her book publications include *Changing Channels: The Prospects for Television in a Digital World* (1998), *Selling Television: British Television in the Global Marketplace* (2004), *European Television Industries* (2005 with P. Iosifidis and M. Wheeler), *Creating Preschool Television* (2010), *The Media and the State* (2016 with T. Flew and P. Iosifidis), *European Media in Crisis* (2015 with J. Trappel and B. Thomass) and *Children's TV and Digital Media in the Arab World* (2017 with Naomi Sakr). She has published widely on UK television exports, European public service broadcasting and the children's media industry. Her work has been funded by the British Academy, the Leverhulme Trust and the Arts and Humanities Research Council.

Lucy Taylor

Lucy is a former primary school teacher specializing in literacy. She has worked in primary schools in the UK and Europe and has a particular interest in children's reading and writing. After studying for a Master's degree in Education she worked as an associate lecturer in Children's Literature at the Open University and as module leader for Primary English on the PGCE course for trainee teachers at the University of Leeds. At present, Lucy is a doctoral researcher funded by the Economic and Social Research Council at the University of Leeds, investigating children's independent writing.

Anne Wood CBE

Anne came to TV via publishing, and could see no reason why children's television should not be of the same quality as a children's book. "Children, their dreams and feelings, their ready enthusiasm, their vulnerability, their essential humanity and their sense of fun" was the inspiration for setting up Ragdoll Productions in 1984. By that time, Anne was already a TV producer of long standing, having produced several award-winning series for Yorkshire TV such as *Ragdolly Anna* and *The Book Tower*. She had also been head of children's at TV-am, producing *Roland Rat* and *Rub-a-dub-tub*. The huge following that developed for these programmes gave Anne an inkling of the gap between children's needs and the provision of good children's television. Since then, Anne has devised and created innovative and pioneering programmes for younger children. All of these programmes fulfil Anne's driving principle: "I want children to be happy inside – in this uncertain world they need to feel secure and loved, only in this way can they grow into confident and creative individuals". The continuing worldwide success of Ragdoll programmes bear witness to the truth of this belief. Anne was awarded a CBE in the 2000 Millennium Queen's Honours List for her services to children's broadcasting.

Karl Woolley

Karl is the managing director of Laughing Gravy Media and has worked in children's television for 20 years. He was managing director of Tell-Tale Productions from 1999 to 2004 in which time the company produced *Tweenies*, *Boo*, and *Fun Song Factory*. He was managing director of Impossible Kids, from 2010 to 2012, when he formed Laughing Gravy Media with Jon Doyle. Whilst working at Impossible Kids, Karl and Jon made 52 episodes of *Buzz and Tell* and 52 episodes of *Fleabag Monkeyface* for CITV. They also secured two new commissions, *Dinopaws* (CBeebies) and *Animattter* (CITV) which are now owned and produced by Laughing Gravy Media.

Lightning Source UK Ltd.
Milton Keynes UK
UKOW07f0430160617
303493UK00006B/21/P